THE MEANINGFUL
WRITING PROJECT

THE MEANINGFUL
WRITING PROJECT

*Learning, Teaching, and Writing
in Higher Education*

MICHELE EODICE
ANNE ELLEN GELLER
NEAL LERNER

UTAH STATE UNIVERSITY PRESS
Logan

Published by Utah State University Press
An imprint of University Press of Colorado
5589 Arapahoe Avenue, Suite 206C
Boulder, Colorado 80303

   The University Press of Colorado is a proud member of
The Association of American University Presses.

The University Press of Colorado is a cooperative publishing enterprise supported,
in part, by Adams State University, Colorado State University, Fort Lewis College,
Metropolitan State University of Denver, Regis University, University of Colorado,
University of Northern Colorado, Utah State University, and Western State Colorado
University.

The paper used in this publication meets the minimum requirements of the American
National Standard for Information Sciences—Permanence of Paper for Printed Library
Materials. ANSI Z39.48-1992

ISBN: 978-1-60732-579-6 (paperback)
ISBN: 978-1-60732-580-2 (ebook)

Library of Congress Cataloging-in-Publication Data

Names: Eodice, Michele, 1957– author. | Geller, Anne Ellen, 1969– author. | Lerner,
    Neal, author.
Title: The meaningful writing project : learning, teaching, and writing in higher educa-
    tion / Michele Eodice, Anne Ellen Geller, Neal Lerner.
Description: Logan : Utah State University Press, [2016] | Includes bibliographical refer-
    ences and index.
Identifiers: LCCN 2016036165 | ISBN 9781607325796 (pbk.) | ISBN 9781607325802
    (ebook)
Subjects: LCSH: English language—Rhetoric—Study and teaching—United States—
    Evaluation. | Report writing—Study and teaching—United States—Evaluation.
Classification: LCC PE1405.U6 E58 2016 | DDC 808/.042071173—dc23
LC record available at https://lccn.loc.gov/2016036165

The University Press of Colorado gratefully acknowledges the generous support of the
University of Oklahoma toward the publication of this book.

Cover image © Lena Bukovsky/Shutterstock

CONTENTS

ACKNOWLEDGMENTS

We would like to thank the 2012 seniors at Northeastern University, St. John's University, and the University of Oklahoma who generously shared their writing experiences with us through our survey and in follow-up interviews. We would also like to thank the faculty from these three institutions who shared their experiences as teachers and writers. This research would also not have been possible without our committed and insightful research teams of undergraduate and graduate students at each of our institutions (see app. D for the complete list). We thank them for sharing our interest in making writing in higher education more meaningful.

Our insights were refined by many thoughtful questions and challenges at presentations and workshops we facilitated together and individually at large and small institutions across the United States with faculty across the disciplines, first-year writing faculty, and the staffs of writing centers. These events gave us many opportunities to hear meaningful writing projects described, and we thank all the participants who shared their experiences with us.

This research would not have been possible without funding from a 2010/11 Conference on College Composition and Communication Research Initiative grant. A Northeastern University Mutual Mentoring Advancement Program grant paid for a crucial writing retreat in January 2016 and supported the creation of this book's infographics. Thanks to Jan Rinehart of NU ADVANCE for this grant support. Insight from Clover Hall and Piyaporn Nawarat of the St. John's Office of Institutional Research was invaluable as we designed this study and especially our student survey, and we thank the St. John's Office of Institutional Research for hosting our student survey. Anne's work on the Meaningful Writing Project has been supported by a 2012 St. John's University Summer Support of Research grant and a spring 2016 research leave. The St. John's Faculty Writing Initiative and faculty writing retreats provided time, space, and scholarly community for thinking and writing about this research. Michele's work was supported by a spring 2015 research leave. And we thank the University Writing Center and the Institute for Writing Studies at St. John's University, Northeastern University English Department, and the OU Writing Center for helping to support our project. Our work was also supported by a publishing subvention offered by the Provost and the Vice President for Research at the University of Oklahoma.

We thank Rosie Ettenheim for her care in designing the infographics in this book and for designing our 2015 CCCC Best Overall Poster (available on the Meaningful Writing Project website: meaningfulwritingproject.net).

Anne would like to thank the undergraduate and graduate students and writing center consultants at St. John's, especially Daniel Dissinger and Christina Migliaecio, as well as English colleagues Steve Sicari, Steve Mentz, Jen Travis, and Harry Denny, for all their support. Thanks to Dorothy Bukay for her administrative support. Many faculty across the disciplines at St. John's, including participants in the Summer Faculty Writing Institutes and the WAC fellows program, followed this research and asked helpful questions along the way. Friends near and far have been very necessary for book writing. Much love and appreciation to Natalie Byfield, who has been with this research and the writing of this book at every stage, and to Theodore Hughes and the extended Geller family, who now know almost as much about what makes writing meaningful as the three of us do and who all rearranged their schedules many times just to accommodate our MWP Skype meetings.

Michele would like to thank the OU Writing Center staff for their support of this study, especially Moira Ozias, Tara Risenhoover, and Donna Benge. Many office assistants and writing consultants lent a hand and shared their thoughts about the project. Several graduate students were closely involved with this project over the years; thanks go to Evan Chambers, J. Michael Rifenburg, Aimee Myers, Rachel Jackson, and Shannon Madden, who was (and is!) our social media and web developer. And, as always, Kami Day was a wonderful partner during this process.

Neal would like to thank students, colleagues and staff at Northeastern for their support and encouragement over the life of this project, particularly Cecelia Musselman, Mya Poe, Chris Gallagher, Beth Britt, Laura Green, Elizabeth Dillon, Linda Collins, and Jean Duddy. Thanks to former Dean Georges Van Den Abbeele for his initial financial support, and special shout-outs to Jess Pauszek and Kyle Oddis for their superb organizational skills and overall good cheer. Thanks to the NEU MSC Nahant Writing Group for the space, support, and motivation to get writing done. The Baker-Lerner clan (Tania, Hannah, Clay, Ezzie, and Violet) made this work both possible and worth doing.

We had such a good experience working with Michael Spooner (USUP) and appreciate all the support from the staff at University Press of Colorado. We would also like to thank Dan Melzer and Rebecca Nowacek, reviewers of our initial draft of this manuscript; their insightful feedback gave us clear direction to strengthen the final version significantly. Anne Herrington offered helpful mentorship. And like many other Utah State University Press authors, we appreciate Kami Day as our copyeditor and Laura Furney's great spirit.

THE MEANINGFUL WRITING PROJECT

Iway inkthay atwhay akesmay away itingwray ojectpray emorablemay orway ean-ingfulmay isway otnay orcingfay udentsstay otay eflectray onway itway utbay oti-vatingmay emthay osay atthay eythay areway inclinedway otay antway otay oday ellway onway ethay ojectpray orfay eirthay ownway enefitbay orway orfay omesay ealray urposepay. Ifway ethay itingwray ojectpray ashay onay eaningmay orway ethay udentstay ashay onlyway away allsmay akestay inway atwhay eythay are-way itingwray aboutway orway ywhay eythay areway itingwray aboutway itway, eythay on'tway eallyray arecay orway aketay itway eriouslysay.

I think what makes a writing project memorable or meaningful is not forcing students to reflect on it but motivating them so that they are inclined to want to do well on the project for their own benefit or for some real purpose. If the writing project has no meaning or the student has only a small stakes in what they are writing about or why they are writing about it they won't really care or take it seriously.

I'veway oneday otslay ofway itingwray atthay Iway avehay eltfay asway ean-ingfulmay, utbay inway ostmay asescay itway asway otnay equiredray ybay ymay ourseworkcay orway ajormay. Osethay itingwray ojectspray aven'thay eltfay ean-ingfulmay ecausebay Iway idn'tday eelfay atthay anyoneway elseway asway oing-gay otay eesay emthay exceptway orfay omesay udentsstay inway ymay assclay orway ethay ofessorpray. Iway aketay itingwray ojectspray atthay areway oinggay otay ebay ublishedpay orway eensay ybay anymay oremay eriouslysay andway eesay emthay asway eingbay oremay eaningfulmay otay emay, ecausebay Iway opehay atthay eythay illway ebay eaningfulmay otay othersway.

I've done lots of writing that I have felt was meaningful, but in most cases it was not required by my coursework or major. Those writing projects haven't felt meaningful because I didn't feel that anyone else was going to see them except for some students in my class or the professor. I take writing projects that are going to be published or seen by many more seriously and see them as being more meaningful to me because I hope that they will be meaningful to others.

PHARMACY AND HEALTH SCIENCE MAJOR
(WHO INCLUDED A LINK TO PIG LATIN
TRANSLATION WEBSITE ALONG WITH HIS SURVEY RESPONSE)

THE MEANINGFUL
WRITING PROJECT

1

THE MEANING OF THE MEANINGFUL WRITING PROJECT

INTRODUCTION—WHY MEANINGFUL WRITING?

> *Normally, I don't have the opportunity to write about a topic I'm inter-*
> *ested in. Also it gave me a chance to be creative with format and wording.*
> —Electrical engineering major

> *I was able to pick a topic that speaks to me related to government on*
> *a personal level as opposed to working toward the professor's topical*
> *expectations.*
> —Government and politics major

> *This is a subject that is important to me and that I chose independently.*
> *Hopefully, this will help me with my future employment as well.*
> —Environmental science major

When asked to describe the most meaningful writing projects they wrote as undergraduates, over seven hundred seniors across three very different institutions—a private, urban Catholic university (undergraduate enrollment: ~15,700); a private, urban university known for experiential learning (undergraduate enrollment: ~17,400); and a public R1 institution (undergraduate enrollment: ~21,000)—told us stories of the powerful roles writing plays in their personal, academic, and professional lives. These stories are at the heart of *The Meaningful Writing Project: Learning, Teaching, and Writing in Higher Education*; our research is grounded in students' experiences and the many ways they make meaning of those experiences.

Our effort to better understand students' meaningful writing experiences draws, in part, on Herrington and Curtis (2000), who recommend that writing researchers "look across writing tasks and across the curriculum at the range of kinds of tasks we set for students, and at how students use this writing" (85). We took up this charge in the primary research questions that motivated our work:

DOI: 10.7330/9781607325802.c001

- What are the qualities of meaningful writing experiences as reported by seniors at three different types of institutions?
- What might students' perceptions of their meaningful writing experiences reveal about students' learning?
- What might faculty who offer the opportunities for students to gain meaningful writing experiences conclude about the teaching of writing in and across the disciplines?

To address these questions, over a two-year period of data collection and another two years of analysis, we engaged in a variety of strategies we describe later in this chapter. Our analysis of the data consisted of identifying patterns of similarity and difference within and across student participants and faculty responses, a grounded-theory approach (Glaser and Strauss 1967) we believe yields new understandings of student learning and the contexts and teaching methods in which it thrives.

In brief, here's what we found: meaningful writing projects offer students opportunities for agency; for engagement with instructors, peers, and materials; and for learning that connects to previous experiences and passions and to future aspirations and identities. Students described the power of personal connection, the thrill of immersion in thought, writing and research, and the satisfaction of knowing the work they produced could be applicable, relevant, and real world. Faculty who teach courses in which meaningful writing takes place often deliberately build these qualities into their teaching and curriculum, expressing their goals and values for writing through specific practices.

We came to these findings through a process at times fraught with methodological, practical, and analytical challenges. But we also felt great excitement as we learned about students' meaningful writing and learning experiences. We will offer a detailed description of our research methods in this chapter, but we want to note here why the concept of meaningfulness is important to us and how we developed it in this project.

Because all three of us are engaged in the enterprise of supporting writing at our universities—and have made careers in doing so, both in writing centers and in writing-across-the-curriculum programs—in designing this project we worked to keep a big-picture question in mind: what kinds of writing experiences are undergraduate students really having? However, rather than collect a list of assignments and students' texts in response to those assignments, we wanted to learn whether undergraduate students found their writing experiences rewarding, instructive, significant, or meaningful.[1] We chose to ask about *meaningful* writing and invited students to name and describe a meaningful writing project even if it had occurred several semesters previous to our asking (and students could offer this description with ease, it seems, although no one had ever asked them before) but also to describe *why* a project was meaningful. This question was remarkably generative. In order to call something *meaningful*, we must have an opportunity to reflect on its significance to us or to make meaning through reflection (Yancey 1998). Over seven hundred students told us they truly understood the question as they focused on what was meaningful for *them*—not for their parents, instructors, or employers.

Students' accounts of meaningful writing run counter to the narratives dominating discussion of higher education—not only currently but historically (e.g., the "Johnny can't write" phenomenon of the 1970s and its periodic reoccurrences). One view is that students are "academically adrift" (Arum and Roksa 2011), reporting less time spent reading and writing than their predecessors, and those who make it to graduation face dim job prospects and crushing levels of student-loan debt (Grafton 2011). At the same time, more and more pressure is on institutions to assess outcomes, whether driven by outside accreditors, legislative mandate, or program improvement.

This strong narrative of crisis and the assessment methodologies used at all levels of education, however, often leave out the study of "incomes" (Guerra 2008) or an understanding of what students bring to their learning experiences and the important meanings they might derive. To date, few studies of students' writing across the disciplines, especially on the scale of what we have done, have made it a concurrent goal to consider how students use (or do not use) those "funds of knowledge" (Moje et al. 2004) or how they "repurpose" out-of-school knowledge (Roozen 2009, 2010) in disciplinary learning and writing.

In terms of book-length studies, Beaufort (2007), Carroll (2002) Herrington and Curtis (2000), Sommers and Saltz (2004), and Sternglass (1997) have each shown in longitudinal research that writing is essential to the ways students form identities as fledgling members of their disciplines. Similarly, Rebecca Nowacek (2011) presents an in-depth study

---

[1] Interestingly, no one thus far in writing studies or English studies has centered their research around meaningfulness, but we did find one reference from *English Journal.* Esther Hess Close (1936) published a two-page set of steps to develop "meaningful communication" and included a step for students to choose themes based on "individual student interests"—an earlier version of what we recommend when we say in a later chapter "tap into personal connection."

of "transfer" for students in a particular interdisciplinary program, but each of these monographs focuses on single institutions or even a single student and does not feature the scope and depth of data we offer. Dan Melzer (2014) investigates writing syllabi and curricular materials from institutions across the United States but does not feature students' perspectives. An online report, the Stanford Study of Writing, led by Andrea Lunsford (2008), does ask questions about students' out-of-school writing, languages, and work experiences, but findings will likely be very different from what we learned from our study's targeted institutions, where significant numbers of the student population are multilingual, international, and/or first-generation college students—many of whom are studying in professional programs such as engineering, pharmacy, legal studies, and nursing. Many of these students live off campus in discourse communities different from, yet closely related to, those they engage in on campus.

Understanding students' writing performance as a developmental process is essential, even when viewing that writing reflectively, as our study does. Previous studies of students' undergraduate writing experiences describe students' relatively uncertain moves from their experience of first-year composition to the disciplinary requirements of writing in their majors (Carroll 2002; Haswell 1991; Hilgers, Hussey, and Stitt-Bergh 1999; Sternglass 1997) and writing postgraduation (Beaufort 2007). Barber, King, and Baxter Magolda (2013) tell us that "developmentally effective experiences [that] respect students' current meaning making and simultaneously invite students to consider new perspectives" (889) lead to faster and stronger gains in self-efficacy, or "self-authorship," as they call it. If the goal of higher education is, in fact, to foster a self-actualization (Maslow 1967), certain personally significant experiences must occur.

We also know the impact of these meaningful experiences extends beyond graduation. In their 2014 report on more than thirty thousand college graduates, *Great Jobs, Great Lives*, researchers found that "well-being" in the workplace was directly related to several undergraduate experiences ("Great Jobs, Great Lives: The 2014 Gallup-Purdue Index Report" 2014). Such engagement was independent of the type of institution: "Where graduates went to college—public or private, small or large, very selective or not selective—hardly matters at all to their current well-being and their work lives in comparison to their experiences in college" (6). Graduates specified undergraduate experiences that contributed most strongly to their current workplace well-being:

- I had at least one professor . . . who made me excited about learning.
- My professors . . . cared about me as a person.
- I had a mentor who encouraged me to pursue my goals and dreams.
- I worked on a project that took a semester or more to complete.
- I had an internship or job that allowed me to apply what I was learning in the classroom.
- I was extremely active in extracurricular activities and organizations while attending [college]. (10)

The first three items are perhaps most relevant to what we report in this book (though many projects students chose as meaningful were semester-long efforts). In terms of those three, Gallup/Purdue ("Great Jobs, Great Lives: The 2014 Gallup-Purdue Index Report" 2014) reports the following: if an employed graduate recalls having "a professor who cared about them as a person," one "who excited them about learning," and if "they had a mentor who encouraged them" to pursue their dreams, the graduate's odds of being engaged at work more than doubled. But only 14% of all college graduates strongly agree that they had support in all three areas" (10).

As we describe in subsequent chapters, students in our study report engagement with instructors and peers, passion for the subjects they wrote about, personal connection with those topics, and a belief that their meaningful writing projects would connect to future writing. In short, meaningful writing completed as an undergraduate may very well produce well-being postgraduation and in a future workplace.

METHODS TO INVESTIGATE STUDENTS' MEANINGFUL WRITING

Rather than marginalize the description of our methods to an appendix, we offer the full story here, not simply to ensure readers that we engaged in RAD research—or what Richard Haswell (2005) describes as research that is replicable, aggregable, and data supported—but to emphasize that in qualitative research of this sort, dispositions of researchers, questions asked, methods of data collection and analysis, and the writing up of that research are intertwined in what Wendy Bishop (1992) describes as "author-saturated texts," or "those that acknowledge their constructedness" (152). What we offer next are the stories of that "constructedness."

STUDY ORIGINS

We began the Meaningful Writing Project almost ten years ago when we were at three different institutions—Clark University (Anne),

Massachusetts Institute of Technology (Neal), and the University of Kansas (Michele). We each had long worked in writing centers and writing-across-the-curriculum programs and had already spent many hours talking about how students experienced writing across their undergraduate years at each of our institutions. In 2004 Anne completed a small pilot study (Geller 2005). Using thirteen short-answer questions, she prompted students to reflect on their experiences reading and writing during their first year. The responses to one question, "Describe a writing assignment from this year that seemed valuable to you. Why do you feel this writing assignment was valuable? (Be specific.)" are reported in "Students' Experiences of Meaning-Centered Writing and Reading" in *Meaning-Centered Education: International Perspectives and Explorations in Higher Education* (Geller 2013).

In 2005 we used that pilot study to develop a Meaningful Writing Project research proposal that looked very much like the research we report on in this book. We applied for a Conference on College Composition and Communication (CCCC) Research Initiative grant that year but did not receive an award, in part, we imagine, because our institutions would not allow us to submit our grant without a very high percentage of costs taken up by grant overhead. After institutional moves to our current positions, we decided we still were committed to the questions of our research and revised our proposal: "Seniors Reflect on Their Meaningful Writing Experiences: A Cross-Institutional Study." We received funding from the 2010–2011 CCCC Research Initiative in January 2011 (and this time our new institutions did not request that we build in overhead costs) and combined this funding with institutional research support and program funds at each of our universities in order to complete surveys and interviews with students and faculty and spend two years on data analysis.

DEVELOPING AND ADMINISTERING THE STUDENT SURVEY

Once we had funding, we knew we did not have enough time to begin our data collection with the graduating class of 2011, so we set out to be ready to survey and interview the class of 2012. From spring 2011 through fall of that year, we developed our survey and IRB protocol. We also had to decide how to delineate seniors. For example, a student could graduate after three years or could be in a five- or six-year undergraduate program. We decided to target students who were on track to graduate with an undergraduate degree in May 2012. At each of our institutions, this group also included students in specialized programs such as the six-year accelerated pharmaceutical doctoral degree.

At the heart of our survey are two open-ended questions (see app. A for the complete survey): "Describe the writing project you found meaningful. What made that project meaningful for you?" However, we also asked students to offer information in several additional areas: (1) a range of demographics (e.g., major and minor, language proficiency, GPA in major and overall); (2) the class in which their meaningful writing project took place, whether that class was in the major, an elective, or a general education requirement, who the instructor of the class was, and when they were enrolled; (3) whether or not they had previously written anything similar to their meaningful writing projects and whether they imagined they would write similar projects in the future (open-ended responses were invited for each of these questions); (4) the ways their experience of their meaningful writing project was or was not in accord with the National Survey of Student Engagement (NSSE) writing questions, which we describe more fully in chapter 3.

Through fall 2011 and spring 2012, the Institutional Research Office at SJU offered feedback on the content of our survey and hosted it online. In fall 2011, we also piloted our survey questions with seniors who were writing center consultants at each of our institutions and then revised the survey questions based on their responses and their reflections on the experience of taking the survey. Determining the best ways to present our multilayered approach to this study (recruiting seniors to complete a survey and be interviewed and asking seniors to name the faculty member we would then invite to take part in the research) to each of our institutional review boards and coordinating IRB approval at three institutions took months. In addition, each of our three institutions disseminates many annual student surveys, especially carefully timed senior surveys, and we had to coordinate the dissemination of our survey within the calendar of those surveys. We invited a total of 10,540 seniors (NEU = 2,414; SJU = 1,982; OU = 6,144) to take the survey from mid-March to mid-April 2012 (see app. B for recruitment e-mail from NEU), and for their participation they were entered in a drawing to receive either a $50 gift card or meal credit.

We closed the senior survey with 780 responses, or a 7.4 percent return rate. After removing partially completed responses, we ended up with 707 surveys, or a final return rate of 6.7 percent. While this rate of response is too low to allow for generalizing to larger populations (a point we take up later in this chapter), the accumulated data from 707 open-ended survey responses was considerable, giving us a great deal to make sense of over the following two years of analysis.

In the process of reading through to make certain we had complete data, we also realized twenty-eight students had gone out of their way to complete the entire survey in order to say they had no meaningful writing projects during their undergraduate careers. We take up the substance of these responses in chapter 2. Also, one complete response was offered in Pig Latin (excerpted in our epigraph)—with a link to an online translation site included in the survey answer.

UNDERGRADUATES AS CO-RESEARCHERS

From the time we conceived of this research, we knew we wanted undergraduates to participate as co-researchers (one of our models was Susan Blum's 2009 method reported in *My Word: Plagiarism and College Culture*). Our reasoning here was that we could think of no better way to capture the perspective of undergraduates—and to value those perspectives— than to have undergraduates play a key role as co-researchers, particularly as interviewers. This was not a matter of our own unease with research interviewing—we've long used that method in our research— but we knew seniors would communicate with their undergraduate peers in ways they would not communicate with us, and our highest priority was to cultivate and honor undergraduates' perspectives.

The first stage of this process was to invite undergraduates to interview the graduating seniors who gave us their follow-up contact information in their survey responses. At SJU, Anne invited writing center consultants to participate. At NEU, Neal recruited undergraduate English majors. At OU, Michele invited students in a first-year seminar focused on undergraduate research. At each of our institutions, we also collaborated with a graduate student who took part in the interview training session and helped coordinate interview times, collected consent forms, and uploaded digitally recorded interviews and reflection sheets (see app. C for a complete list of undergraduate and graduate researchers who took part). We asked the undergraduates who volunteered to complete an IRB training module for certification, read two short qualitative research articles about interviewing (Bogdan and Biklen 2006; Seidman 1998), and come to a group training session for which we compensated them for their time. In that session we discussed the readings, and then we either asked the undergraduates to interview one another in pairs using our shared protocol (see app. D) or we asked one pair to complete an interview observed by the group. In both versions, we closed with reflection on the process and feedback on the interview questions, which led us to make several changes for the final version of the questions.

Our undergraduate researchers all told us they appreciated the opportunity to talk with their peers about meaningful writing projects from across the disciplines. Often they were surprised by what their peers told them. What was interesting about the OU interviews was that because the interviewers were first-year students and the interviewees were seniors, the seniors often had to explain their projects. In one interview, for example, a senior describes a semester-long project, and on mentioning "lit review" as a component, notices the first-year student interviewer doesn't seem familiar with the genre:

> *Hank:* It was actually more structured . . . I guess there are different forms that academic essays can take. This was more of the formal kind where you do a lit review. Are you familiar with a lit review?
> *Andre:* Vaguely.
> *Hank:* A lit review is an overview of the current theories and academic discussions going on over the topic. I was doing securitization of borders in Europe. So I looked up what all the different authors had said over securitization. What securitization means. The history of it. That was actually the hardest part.

But moments of surprise arose even among the interviews being led by experienced writing center consultants. For example, in one of the SJU interview recordings we offer in greater detail later, we hear the interviewer's surprise that the meaningful writing project was worth just 5 percent of the student's semester grade.

Our undergraduate research team members completed twenty-seven interviews at our three institutions. The data set from these interviews includes digitally recorded interviews, transcripts of the interviews, some assignments, some drafts of the meaningful writing projects, and the interviewers' reflections on the interviews.

ANALYZING THE STUDENT-SURVEY DATA

Faced with a large amount of survey data, much of it open-ended responses, we decided to ground the bulk of our analysis in the "Why was your writing project meaningful?" question. As soon as we started to read through the responses, we saw and heard striking evidence of students explaining how their writing and their learning (about course content, about themselves, about their disciplines and future professions) were interconnected. We chose the emic path rather than the etic approach that imposes an existing frame first. One definition of emic seems especially fitting for our study: "Emic constructs are accounts, descriptions, and analyses expressed in terms of the conceptual schemes and categories regarded as meaningful and appropriate by the native members whose beliefs and behaviors are being studied' (Lett 1990, 130; see also Hass and Osborn 2007). In early summer 2012, we worked with randomly chosen sets of responses to develop codes we saw emerging and reoccurring (see app. E for list of codes). Our development of codes is in accord with what Johnny Saldaña (2015) describes:

> A code in qualitative inquiry is most often a word or short phrase that symbolically assigns a summative, salient, essence-capturing, and/or evocative attribute for a portion of language-based or visual data. . . . Just as a title represents and captures a book or film or poem's primary content and essence, so does a code represent and capture a datum's primary content and essence. (4)

We then made a number of attempts to code independently and establish interrater reliability so we could each more quickly code portions of the 707 survey responses. However, we could never get better than 75 percent interrater reliability. While this might speak to flaws in our research design or our own weaknesses as researchers, we quickly came to realize that while some survey responses were short, like this one—"It made me realize how little power the average American actually has" (code: *content learning*)—other responses were long and rich and required multiple codes:

> It was about a research study in which I participated for summer 2011. It took me almost three weeks to write that paper as it was 26 pages long. First time, I applied all the material learned in the Research Methods class such as, formulating hypothesis, writing introduction and method section, analyzing data, etc. to a real life situation. I was very excited writing that paper because it was based upon a real research study, carried out at St. John's University, in which I directly worked with human participants and analyzed data. Although, we couldn't get all of our results significant but at least some of them were, and it was a big accomplishment for me and my research buddy. (codes: *length, affect, transfer, accomplishment, app+*)

From our realization about the complexity of what we came to call the "*Why meaningful?*" responses and our desire to ground this study in what we could learn from students about why they had found these named projects to be their most meaningful, we decided to code every one of the 707 responses collaboratively. That meant talking through our rationale for the codes we were using and prioritizing the three or four most significant reasons/codes for why the project had been meaningful.

Thus began approximately a year of almost weekly Skype sessions in which we coded together for up to two hours at a time. While the time invested in this step seems almost unfathomable now, it did lead to the three of us living with our data, engaging in what Peter Smagorinsky (2008) recommends: "The flexible and generative nature of the collaborative approach [is] more likely to produce an insightful reading of the data because each decision is the result of a serious and thoughtful exchange about what to call each and every data segment" (402). To ensure consistency, after nearly completing all of our coding, we pulled a random sample of previously coded data and coded again. We found nearly 100 percent agreement between the two coding sessions many months apart.

ANALYZING STUDENT INTERVIEWS

In preparing some of our first presentations from this study, we turned to the student interviews to fill out our understanding of the contexts of students' meaningful writing experiences in ways the survey alone could not provide. From those interviews, we were able to learn about students' larger writing lives and experiences, the courses in which the meaningful writing projects were written, and the relationship of these to students' identity, undergraduate experiences, and self-professed goals. We began to present individual students in first-person narrative case studies (Yin 2013), and in doing so, we were also able to start seeing the weight of some of our codes and the interconnection among other codes. In addition, as we worked with the interviews, we learned more detail about students' experiences in their courses, and we heard more about their relationships with their faculty. This information informed how we went on to adjust the faculty-data stage of our research.

SURVEYING AND INTERVIEWING FACULTY

We had always planned to interview the faculty who were named as having assigned and supported students' meaningful writing projects (and we had IRB approval to do so), but we realized as soon as we received the seniors' surveys that we could never interview all the faculty who were named. Somehow, we had expected a smaller number of faculty to be named several times, but seniors instead named many faculty only once, with just a few exceptions of faculty who were named by several students, often for the same course. As a result, we decided to develop a survey to capture more faculty descriptions of teaching with writing, which meant we wrote IRB modifications that had, once again, to clear the institutional review boards at each of our institutions. We knew from our years of work with faculty that the survey would have to be short if we wanted a strong response rate, so we worked to develop a two-question survey with a request that faculty give us their contact information if they were willing to be interviewed. We piloted the initial version of our faculty survey with a small group of faculty who had been involved with WAC programming at OU and SJU but who had not been named in the students' surveys, and then we made adjustments to our questions based on feedback from that pilot. The final version of the survey consisted of the following questions:

1. We're sending you this survey because a student named a writing project written for your course as the most meaningful of their undergraduate career. Why do think that was so?

2. Please tell us about how writing "works" in your teaching—what is its role in terms of what you want your students to learn, where does it occur within the semester, and what does the instruction you provide look like (in assignments, in feedback, in class/lab, in office hours)?

We also knew that to get as large a number of responses as we wanted, our request and invitation would have to be complimentary, which wasn't difficult because in our e-mail solicitations to faculty we told the truth as we had it from the student survey:

> Dear Professor X: I am writing to you because a student participating in a cross-institutional study I am conducting—Seniors Reflect on Their Meaningful Writing Experiences—cited an assignment written in one of your classes as one of their most meaningful writing experiences. The course was XXX taught in Semester/Year. Below is a description of the assignment: XXX. To learn more about this assignment as well as how you design writing assignments and teach with writing, I invite you to participate in a three question online survey.

Some faculty were surprised they had been named as *most meaningful.* Other faculty were not at all surprised. In fact, some faculty had an "of course" response—either because of their confidence in their curriculum and pedagogy or because students had been telling them for years that this particular assignment was meaningful. We offered faculty three options for completing the survey: (1) anonymously, (2) with their names but not an offer to take part in an interview, or (3) with an indication that they were willing to take part in a follow-up interview. We sent out 382 invitations (NEU = 100; OU = 210; SJU = 72) to individual faculty and received 160 completed faculty surveys (a 42 percent return rate); 134 faculty agreed to be contacted for follow-up interviews, and our undergraduate team eventually conducted interviews with 60 total faculty.

ANALYZING FACULTY-SURVEY RESPONSES

Because the first faculty-survey response was a reflection on the meaningful writing project the student had named ("We're sending you this survey because a student named a writing project written for your course as the most meaningful of their undergraduate career. Why do think that was so?"), and we wanted to maintain a focus on exploring meaningful writing projects from students' perspectives even as we considered faculty responses, we coded the response to the first question with the codes developed from students' "Why meaningful?" responses. What is interesting is that sometimes, even when it is clear the student and faculty are describing exactly the same assignment, the "Why meaningful?" codes we assigned are different. For example, from a class on race, gender and the media:

- Student response to survey question 1, which first asked them to describe the project: "I was asked to discuss my family history and genealogy. I found it to be very meaningful, because I learned stuff about my family that I didn't know before. I was also able to discuss stories that had been passed down through generations." Response to the second part of the question, which asked why the project was meaningful: "It was nice to have time to reflect on what I had learned about my family." (codes: *reflection, content learning, time*)
- Corresponding faculty response to survey question 1: "The assignment asked students to make connections between their family stories and their personal identities. I think students may find value in this assignment because they are invited to define themselves against the tapestry of family background in unique ways—race, gender & class. Students interview their family members as part of their work and engage in important conversations that they otherwise might miss." (codes: *personal connection, researching to learn*)

But, as is also obvious here, even though *personal connection* is not a code we used for the "Why meaningful?" portion of the student's answer, it's clear in the student's first survey question answer that the project was related to the student's own "family history and genealogy."

In other cases, as with a meaningful writing project written in an all-online course, Decision Making, the student and faculty descriptions of the project were similar, but our codes were still slightly different.

- Student response to survey question 1: "A ten page assignment that required presenting three different scenarios to solve a problem. . . . The project was meaningful to me because I used a real-life work situation to base my paper on. The writing project gave me the chance to explore three different scenarios to solve this work situation and led to a better working environment for me." (codes: *app+*, *personal connection*)˙

- Corresponding faculty response to survey question 1: "The assignment is a course spanning task that seeks to create a real world experience in strategic thinking and problem solving that is focused on issues in the future. Each phase is completed and feedback is given as the unit topics are covered. The assignment is designed to provide flexibility in topics and opportunity for creative thinking. This assignment allows the student to reflect on issues they are passionate about, and think strategically about possible resolutions outcomes." (codes: *app+*, *reflection*, *process*)

The second faculty-survey question offered different data given its more general focus on how writing played a role in the faculty member's teaching, and we spent quite a bit of time in person in Boston on a three-day data-analysis retreat struggling to determine how to best code these responses while still staying true to our "Why was the project most meaningful to students?" lens. We first tried to use the same codes we had used for students' "Why meaningful?" responses and for faculty members' descriptions of the learning and teaching of the meaningful writing projects, but we allowed ourselves to add new, additional codes, and we could agree on some of these (*synthesis* and *reading*) when we worked with a set of responses separately and then brought our analysis together. However, we realized how familiar much of what faculty described in that second response seemed to us; over and over again, we heard faculty describe their goals, their biases, and their familiar WAC/WID practices such as peer review or feedback or drafts or in-class minilessons. We asked ourselves what seemed to be important, and when we talked that through, using a set of responses, we came to see that we could easily separate these practices from beliefs faculty expressed about writing, from values faculty articulated, and from goals faculty were trying to reach with the assignments and learning and teaching they described using in their courses. We also developed a code for instances of faculty describing teaching out of what they knew from their own experiences writing and researching: teacher as writer. Once again, we spent several months via Skype collaboratively coding these faculty-survey responses. While we do not report on the specific results of this coding in chapter 5 when we focus on faculty data, it did inform our shaping of the case studies in that chapter, particularly instances in which faculty and student values and goals for writing were and were not aligned.

INTERVIEWING FACULTY

To interview the faculty, we had to prepare three new sets of undergraduate interviewers because most of our previous interviewers had graduated. This time, Anne and Michele asked for volunteers from among their writing centers' staffs, Neal once again invited undergraduate English majors to take part, and we again compensated student researchers for their time. We each used the same process we had used when we prepared those who interviewed the seniors (IRB certification, the same readings, a practice session), as well as a shared interview protocol (see app. F). This time each of us asked one of the undergraduate interviewers to complete an actual interview with a faculty member who had been named in a student survey in a "fishbowl" setting with the other interviewers watching, listening, and taking notes. Afterward, we led a debrief of that interview as a way of preparing the group members for their own interviews. As we noted above, student perspective was our driving force; we knew faculty would speak to us quite differently than they would to undergraduates, some of whom were familiar with their courses and some of whom were not. Certainly, in both instances faculty would be performing in a particular rhetorical situation, but as we listened to completed interviews and heard faculty explaining their histories with teaching writing and as writers, the ways writing played a role in their courses, and their hopes for student learning through writing, we were struck repeatedly by the honesty, frankness, and, at times, fragility of faculty experiences. We do not imagine faculty would have been similarly open describing their experiences to fellow faculty, particularly ones they might see as "experts" on the teaching of writing.

PRESENTING OUR RESEARCH

Throughout this research and writing process, we developed conference and invited-workshop presentations. These talks provided points at which we pushed ourselves to more certain analysis. Our earliest presentations after we coded the student responses led us to our most frequent codes for the "Why meaningful?" responses: *personal connection, app+, content learning, researching to learn.* And identifying the prevalence of these codes provided a lens for analyzing our data in smaller and/or more focused ways—co-occurrences of these codes and co-occurrences of these codes with other less frequent codes. The 2014 International Writing Across the Curriculum Conference was the first time we wrote and presented first-person faculty narratives developed from faculty interviews, and our (award-winning!) poster presentation at the 2015 Conference on College Composition and Communication (CCCC) was the first time we presented the most frequent codes of the student responses to the "Why meaningful?" question next to the most frequent codes of the faculty responses to "Why do you think this was a student's most meaningful writing project"?

Another data-collection effort launched at our 2015 CCCC Poster Session was to capture CCCCs attendees' meaningful writing experiences as undergraduates, as well as to create a link on our project website (http://meaningfulwritingproject.net) for anyone to contribute descriptions of the most meaningful writing projects they completed as undergraduates and why they chose those projects as most meaningful. Once again, we navigated the somewhat choppy waters of multi-institutional IRB approval but ultimately received permission to collect data at these additional sites. We invite readers of this book to contribute your stories: http://tinyurl.com/meaningfulWP.

A BROAD LOOK AT STUDY PARTICIPANTS

In the individual chapters that follow, we present specific findings from surveys and interviews and discuss those findings in relation to key current concepts in learning and teaching writing. Before we offer those specifics, however, in this section, we present an overview of student and faculty demographics, highlighting some of the institutional similarities and differences.

INSTITUTIONAL PROFILES

Our participants were all students and faculty (full and part time) at Northeastern University, the University of Oklahoma, or St. John's University at the time of this research study. Our undergraduate and graduate co-researchers were enrolled students at these institutions. The following infographic chapter describes characteristics of each institution for the academic year in which we collected our student data. Although our 707 student-survey participants represent a small percentage of all enrolled undergraduates at our three institutions during the 2011–2012 academic year, the Common Data Set (CDS) from each of our schools for that year provides an overview of the institutional context (or at least the one publicly reported in the CDS). We offer these data to provide that context, as well as to point to institutional differences in terms of the data represented in the CDS. We do not claim that our student participants are representative of all students in US higher education or our overall student populations. However, we do believe that the context we offer in the infographic chapter (which follows chapter 1) speaks to aspects of the campus climate in which our students' meaningful writing projects were situated.

There are additional differences among our schools. While the University of Oklahoma is public, Northeastern and St. John's are private. St. John's is religiously affiliated: Catholic and Vincentian. The University of Oklahoma sits in a small college town, and while both Northeastern and St. John's have quite large campuses, they are located in urban cities. Northeastern is perhaps best known for its "co-op" program, or a long-standing experiential learning component in which nearly all students complete from one to three six-month, full-time (and usually paid) work experiences during their tenure. As a result, most NEU undergraduates take five full years to graduate. St. John's has the largest percentage of students of color of the three institutions, while Oklahoma has the largest percentage of Native American students. While none of the three institutions has a full account of students' languages, spoken and written, we imagine from our experience on the ground that St. John's, which is located in one of the most linguistically diverse counties in the country, is the most diverse when it comes to multilingual writers and speakers, while Northeastern has the largest percentage of international undergraduates (we realize, of course, that not all international students are multilingual).

STUDENT-SURVEY PARTICIPANT DEMOGRAPHICS

As we show in the infographic chapter, student-survey participants were divided pretty much by the student populations of our institutions. Differences in reported race/ethnicity were also reflective of our overall student populations: the majority of participants from SJU identified as students of color, while OU had the largest percentage of Native American participants. In terms of gender, we were somewhat surprised to see female participants outnumber males by more than two to one even though the overall ratio at our institutions is approximately fifty/fifty. Perhaps females are more willing to fill out surveys, or perhaps they are more likely to have meaningful writing experiences. The latter conclusion is supported by research from the National Survey of Student Engagement (NSSE), which shows that women undergraduates are more likely to report being engaged than men (Kuh 2003). The age differences are also a function of our

Psychology	41
Pharmacy	21
Administrative Leadership	18
Public Relations	17
English	15
Accounting	14
Biology	14
Chemical Engineering	14
Political Science	12
Mechanical Engineering	11
Behavioral Engineering	11
Criminal Justice	10
Zoology	10
History	9
International Affairs	9
Liberal Studies	9
Sociology	9

Figure 1.1. Most frequently named STEM majors.

institutional differences, such as NEU's seniors largely being in their fifth year (and thus twenty-two or older) and the presence of nontraditionally aged students at OU.

It is interesting to note that 40 percent of the 707 seniors identified themselves as being proficient in reading, writing, or speaking a language other than English and that this percentage is also fairly consistent across the participants from all three institutions.

In terms of students' majors, for all participants, the most frequently cited major was psychology (see figure 1.1), perhaps an indication that psychology majors frequently give and take surveys. The array of frequently named majors from social science, STEM, and humanities fields also offers an indication that our findings are applicable to a wide range of students (see figure 1.2).

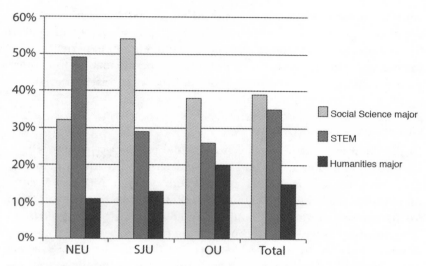

Figure 1.2. Frequently named majors from social science, STEM, and humanities.

BUT IS IT GENERALIZABLE?

We do not intend to argue in this book that student and faculty experiences in our home universities are the same as student and faculty experiences in every US institution—or even that the students who participated in our study are representative of our institutions, given our relatively low survey response rate and that our study design did not rely on random sampling. But we do believe the conclusions and theories we offer may be applicable to learning and teaching contexts at any college or university. We are left even more certain of this conclusion because of the ways faculty and staff at a wide variety of institutions—other public and private universities, regional universities, small private colleges, community colleges, technical universities—have received our findings as we have offered dozens of workshops and presentations over the last several years. Those audiences have found student and faculty experiences and explanations of meaningfulness both familiar and inspiring. As we present our work in these varied settings, we always ask participants to write about and share their meaningful writing projects completed as undergraduates (and we also continue to ask graduate students and undergraduates at our own institutions to respond to this prompt). We are consistently struck by how the responses represent the themes we saw repeated in our students' data. In other words, across widely different contexts and over extended periods of time, people can recall a key meaningful writing project from their undergraduate experiences and describe that meaning making in similar terms. We believe the meaningful writing project is a shared phenomenon, one deeply enmeshed in our experiences of schooling in this country and in our experiences with writing and writing instruction (and it would be fascinating to explore these questions in contexts outside of the US educational system).

OUTLINE OF THIS BOOK

In the chapters that follow, we present the results we gathered from student and faculty surveys and interviews along with additional materials we collected, including interviewers' written reflections completed after each interview. Immediately following this introduction we have inserted an infographic chapter that can be referred back to as you read this book. We build chapters 2–4 around terms we see as key to current discussions of student writing and learning—*agency*, *engagement*, and *learning for transfer*—and in each chapter, we situate our research within the literature in those areas. In these chapters, we offer case studies, drawing from student interviews, to offer depth and nuance to the concepts we discuss. In chapter 5, we triangulate our findings from the student data with what we learned from faculty-survey responses and interviews and also offer several brief case studies across a range of disciplines and types of classes in which the meaningful writing projects took place. Finally, our last chapter offers what we see are the implications and applications from our study for research and teaching.

CHAPTER 2: AGENCY

Kathleen Blake Yancey (2011, 416) describes the question "how might we define agency?" as "at the heart of rhetoric and likewise at the heart of the teaching enterprise." In our analysis of student-survey results, we saw a clear pattern emerge in terms of how particular writing assignments—and often the acts of faculty to shape and deliver those assignments—resulted in students making note of a particular kind of agency. More specifically, most frequently co-occurring with our codes for why students chose a project as meaningful was that it *allowed* or gave them the opportunity to pursue a subject or write in a particular form. However, there was a clear limit for many students to this freedom, as an equally frequent co-occurrence with our codes was students remarking that an instructor or writing task *required* or *forced* them into some action. And, at times, these qualities showed up together.

Agency, then, in the perspective of students participating in our research, consists of the opportunity to pursue subjects one is passionate about or writing relevant to a professional aspiration or future pursuit. However, such opportunity is shaped by instruction and by the writing task itself. After all, the writing tasks students were reporting on were often required assignments in required classes (the latter made up 56 percent of courses students named). Still, within such requirements, students have opportunities to find meaning in their writing projects and, further, to develop a sense of agency about themselves as writers, learners, and thinkers.

CHAPTER 3: ENGAGEMENT

In *Making the Most of College*, Richard Light (2004) describes the ways students' writing is a key contributor to their sense of engagement with course material and with peers and faculty. Similarly, we saw repeatedly in our survey and interview results students describing new writing tasks or new ways of learning coupled with an investigation of a topic that offered high interest or personal connection (and, thus, motivation). The result represented a unique opportunity for our students, one in which they were engaged with their learning and their writing.

Light's definition of engagement, connected closely to the time and effort students devote to their studies, represents one dimension of what we saw happening in students' accounts of their meaningful writing projects. Following George D. Kuh (2009) and the National Survey of Student Engagement (NSSE), we describe how "time and effort" were factors in students' choice of their meaningful writing project, and we compare the results of our survey with results from the NSSE (2012) topical module on students' "experiences with writing" from the same year as our survey, 2012. We also explore the social view of engagement and discuss what we learned about how students engage with others (peers and instructors) as well as with *things* or nonhuman actors (subject matter or content) to make meaning through their writing.

CHAPTER 4: LEARNING FOR TRANSFER

While in our student survey, we did not ask about transfer per se—at least directly—our methods provide powerful means to understand how undergraduates across the disciplines make meaning from their writing projects, what previous experiences influence that meaning, and how students expect that meaning to contribute or transfer forward to future writing. In this chapter we shift the conversation from *teaching for transfer* to *learning for transfer* as we put our findings in relation to writing studies transfer research and call for a focus on what students bring to and take from their learning rather than how they do or do not respond to transfer-intentioned curricula.

CHAPTER 5: MEANINGFUL WRITING HAPPENS WHEN . . .

Students' meaningful writing projects tell us a great deal about how students learn to write, but they also tell us a great deal about how writing is taught. In this chapter we draw on faculty survey and interview results to focus on those teaching practices and assignments that resulted in meaningful learning, and we distill, as much as possible, the common qualities these practices share. We saw a wide range of assignments in a wide range of disciplines, in both required and elective courses, all leading to students' most meaningful writing projects. Such range speaks to writing assignments as vital tools in the larger processes of learning and teaching, as well as to models of structuring student learning applicable to a large variety of contexts. Overall, faculty survey responses and interviews show us that pedagogy comes in multiple forms and through multiple channels and that faculty care a great deal about students' processes of writing as well as their products.

CHAPTER 6: SOME CONCLUSIONS

While we resist reducing our findings in this book to a template or formula that would guarantee students produce meaningful writing, we offer in this chapter some lessons for learning and teaching we feel are applicable to multiple sites of instruction. Meaningful writing projects that enable student agency, engage students with others and with content, and offer opportunities to learn for transfer have the qualities of personal connection, applicability, and immersion in processes of research and writing while balancing required elements and student choice. Not all these qualities happen at once or even all together, but their presence more often than not ensured that students found a writing project meaningful, worth recounting in a survey and remembering for its significance in their own lives. And it seems those desirable elements listed above are more likely to appear when placed within an expansive frame for learning.

INFOGRAPHICS

RESEARCH TIMELINE

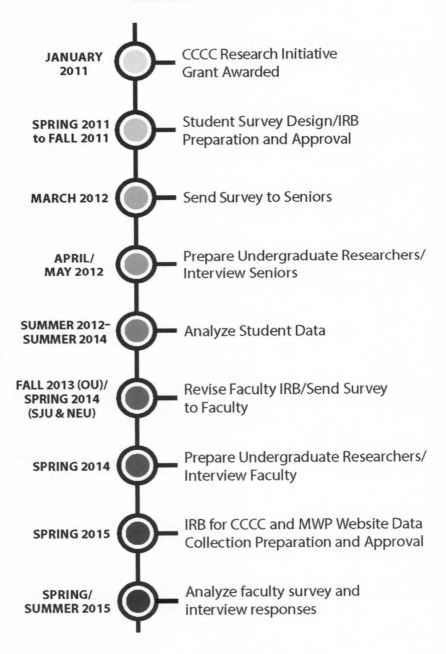

JANUARY 2011	CCCC Research Initiative Grant Awarded
SPRING 2011 to FALL 2011	Student Survey Design/IRB Preparation and Approval
MARCH 2012	Send Survey to Seniors
APRIL/ MAY 2012	Prepare Undergraduate Researchers/ Interview Seniors
SUMMER 2012– SUMMER 2014	Analyze Student Data
FALL 2013 (OU)/ SPRING 2014 (SJU & NEU)	Revise Faculty IRB/Send Survey to Faculty
SPRING 2014	Prepare Undergraduate Researchers/ Interview Faculty
SPRING 2015	IRB for CCCC and MWP Website Data Collection Preparation and Approval
SPRING/ SUMMER 2015	Analyze faculty survey and interview responses

707 surveys from seniors at 3 schools

27 one-to-one interviews with seniors

160 surveys from faculty who taught the classes in which students wrote their meaningful writing project

60 one-to-one interviews with faculty

	CARNEGIE CLASSIFICATION	NUMBER OF UNDERGRADUATES	ANNUAL TUITION
NEU	RU/H	16,385	$37,840
SJU	DRU	11,390	$33,125
OU	RU/VH	17,787	$7,914

	NEU	SJU	OU
ADMITTANCE RATE	35%	32%	81%
6-YEAR GRADUATION RATE	77%	58%	68%

PARTICIPANTS BY RACE

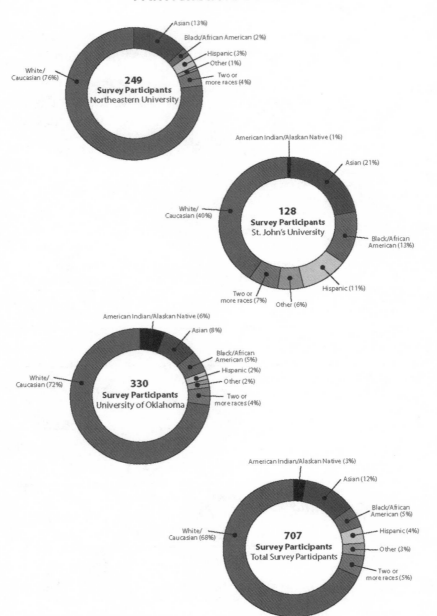

Asian (13%)
Black/African American (2%)
Hispanic (3%)
Other (1%)
Two or more races (4%)
White/Caucasian (76%)

249
Survey Participants
Northeastern University

American Indian/Alaskan Native (1%)
Asian (21%)
White/Caucasian (40%)
Black/African American (13%)
Two or more races (7%)
Other (6%)
Hispanic (11%)

128
Survey Participants
St. John's University

American Indian/Alaskan Native (6%)
Asian (8%)
Black/African American (5%)
Hispanic (2%)
Other (2%)
Two or more races (4%)
White/Caucasian (72%)

330
Survey Participants
University of Oklahoma

American Indian/Alaskan Native (3%)
Asian (12%)
Black/African American (5%)
Hispanic (4%)
Other (3%)
Two or more races (5%)
White/Caucasian (68%)

707
Survey Participants
Total Survey Participants

PARTICIPANTS BY AGE

Northeastern University

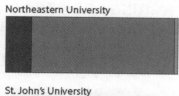

St. John's University

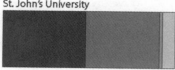

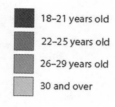

- 18–21 years old
- 22–25 years old
- 26–29 years old
- 30 and over

University of Oklahoma

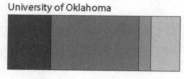

Total Survey Participants

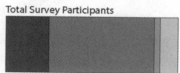

PARTICIPANTS BY GENDER

Northeastern University

69%
Female

27%
Male

University of Oklahoma

65%
Female

33%
Male

St. John's University

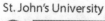
69%
Female

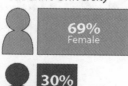
30%
Male

Total Survey Participants

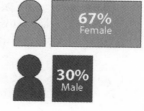
67%
Female

30%
Male

SENIORS' READING, WRITING OR SPEAKING PROFIENCY IN LANGUAGES(S) OTHER THAN ENGLISH

38%
Northeastern
University

41%
St. John's
University

41%
University of
Oklahoma

40%
Total

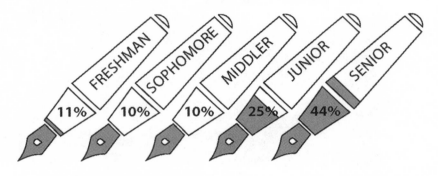

11% FRESHMAN 10% SOPHOMORE 10% MIDDLER 25% JUNIOR 44% SENIOR

NEARLY HALF THE STUDENTS SURVEYED WROTE THEIR MWP
IN THEIR SENIOR YEAR

52%
wrote their MWP
in their major

17%
wrote their MWP in
an elective course

29%
wrote their MWP in a
general education course

52%
wrote their MWP in
a required course

For the project you've described as meaningful, had you previously written anything similar?

For the project you've described as meaningful, are there ways in which this writing project might contribute to the kinds of writing you hope to do in the future?

WHY MEANINGFUL? STUDENT RESPONSES

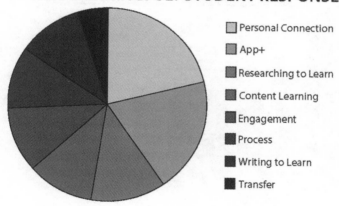

- Personal Connection
- App+
- Researching to Learn
- Content Learning
- Engagement
- Process
- Writing to Learn
- Transfer

MORE THAN 1 IN 3 STUDENTS
DESCRIBED PERSONAL CONNECTION AS A REASON THAT THEIR PROJECT WAS MEANINGFUL

WHY MEANINGFUL VARIED BY WHEN WRITTEN

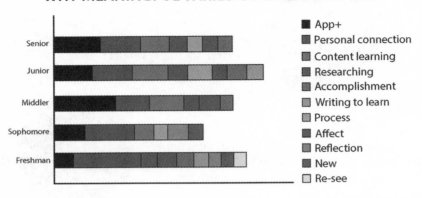

Legend:
- App+
- Personal connection
- Content learning
- Researching
- Accomplishment
- Writing to learn
- Process
- Affect
- Reflection
- New
- Re-see

Categories (left axis): Senior, Junior, Middler, Sophomore, Freshman

WHY MEANINGFUL BY GENDER

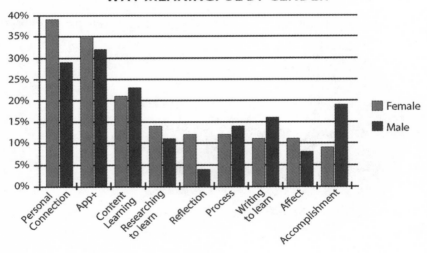

Y-axis: 0% to 40% (in 5% increments)

X-axis categories: Personal Connection, App+, Content Learning, Researching to learn, Reflection, Process, Writing to learn, Affect, Accomplishment

Legend: Female, Male

28 STUDENTS WENT OUT OF THEIR WAY TO SAY THEY HAD NO MEANINGFUL WRITING AS UNDERGRADS

2
AGENCY AND THE MEANINGFUL WRITING PROJECT

As a student who is passionate about the environment, I was able to research in depth the actions that had been taken to respond to the issue, and to discuss the plans of officials to deal with the issue in the future. Not only was my paper relevant to my interests, but I was able to gain a better understanding of the workings of real-world agencies set up to deal with similar issues.

—Environmental geology major

We chose agency as one of our frameworks (along with engagement and learning for transfer) for exploring meaningful writing projects for two primary reasons: (1) as we analyzed why students told us their writing projects were meaningful, we repeatedly saw the ways in which students described opportunities or freedom to pursue topics of interest, to connect those topics to what they had passion for or had experienced, and to map their meaningful writing projects to their future writing and professional identities—as the student quote above describes. In addition, the agency students experienced with their meaningful writing projects was often offered in contrast to the rest of their schooling; (2) the development of student agency is a long-standing theme in writing and literacy studies and in education literature more generally, and deservedly so: having students gain control of their writing and actively constructing their learning is an important goal, but it is an elusive goal amidst the challenges of the social and material conditions they face.

There are multiple viewpoints from which to see and know agency.

In his work on transformative learning, John M. Dirkx (1998) has noted, "To be meaningful, what is learned has to be viewed as personally significant in some way; it must feel purposive and illuminate qualities and values of importance to the person" (9). The students in our study describe their meaningful writing projects similarly, and our most frequent codes of *personal connection* and *app+* are reflected in Dirkx's quotation above as "personally significant" and "feel purposive." What

DOI: 10.7330/9781607325802.c002

is offered in an assignment is taken up by students when they recognize they have "the capacity for action . . . the capacity to critically shape their own responsiveness" to a given situation. This "capacity that works upon the self" is also a definition of agency (Emirbayer and Mische 1998, 971).

This internal-versus-external debate over where agency might be initiated (i.e., starting with the learner versus starting with the teacher) is key to understanding student agency in educational contexts. We align ourselves with Marilyn Cooper's (2011) definition of agency as "an emergent property of embodied individuals" (421); agency is embodied, not generated and internalized from external action, but, according to Jane Bennett (2001), "instead is based in individuals' lived knowledge that their actions are their own" (155). Many students who participated in our study chose to reflect on a writing experience that confirmed that their actions were their own. Yet we, like Shari Stenberg (2015), resist seeing agency through the neoliberal lens in which "agency valorizes individualism, the subject who acts alone in service of individual gain and efficacy" and instead advocate for what Stenberg calls a "located agency that ultimately involves a turn toward others" (119). This "turn toward others" is prevalent in classes in which writing plays a central role, and agency is best defined as a result of social interactions among instructors, peers, and subject matter, all taking place within a matrix of identity and subject formation, and cognitive and social development, and infused with power and authority.

In educational contexts, students' development of agency is also situated within a continuum of the long-standing function of education to replicate status-quo hierarchies or to offer opportunities to transform the status quo. Writing courses have long been positioned at various places on this continuum, whether the view is first-year writing courses as barriers to full participation (e.g., Berlin 1987; Crowley 1998) or upper-division writing courses as contexts in which students develop "discursive identities" aligned with their future aspirations (e.g., Poe, Lerner, and Craig 2010). Evidence from longitudinal studies of students' writing development offers a far more nuanced view, with writing courses or, more accurately, disciplinary courses that contain significant writing components acting as both hurdles and opportunities (e.g., Beaufort 2007; Carroll 2002; Herrington and Curtis 2000; Leki 2007; Lillis 2002; Sternglass 1997). Still, we cannot help but think of Melzer's 2014 study of writing assignments across the curriculum in which the preponderance of writing students encountered was largely "knowledge-telling" tasks or relatively brief written responses in exam contexts. In these situations, in which the assignments stand pretty low on the ladder of

Bloom's Taxonomy, we doubt much meaningful writing occurs. Thus, the impulse for us to foster agency is ever challenged by the inherently "reproductive" nature of schools and school-based writing (Hull and Katz 2006, 44).

When it comes to creating conditions for student agency to be possible, Moje and Lewis (2007) describe these:

> Opportunity to learn . . . requires that participants have the space and support for agentic action, that is, that learners have opportunities to make and remake themselves, their identities, their discursive toolkits, and their relationships on the basis of the new ideas, practices, or discourses learned through their participation in a learning activity. (20)

As we show in this chapter, students' sense of meaningfulness *was* a particular kind of agency rooted in "new ideas, practices, or discourses learned through their participation in a learning activity," namely their meaningful writing projects. In other words, our claim is that students' perception that their writing is meaningful is also a perception of that writing experience as agentive.

We also must note that a surprising number of students (twenty-eight, or 4 percent of all those who completed the survey) chose not simply to ignore our invitation to tell us about their meaningful writing experiences but instead filled out the entire survey, only to report that they had *not* had any such experiences:

> I haven't found any of my writing projects meaningful. They were always about something that did not necessarily interest me. Most of the time my assignments included a prompt or business that I needed to write about.

Within these "not meaningful" responses, we can see the elements that were in place for other students, and by contrasting *not meaningful* with *meaningful*, we can understand something about the conditions necessary for students to achieve agency.

Agency, from the perspective of students participating in our research, consists of opportunities to pursue matters they are passionate about and/or to write something relevant to a professional aspiration or future pursuit. However, such opportunities are shaped by instruction and by the writing task itself. After all, the writing tasks students reported on were often required assignments in required classes (the latter made up 56 percent of courses students named). Still, within such parameters, a space was created to allow students to find meaning in their writing projects and, further, to develop a sense of agency about themselves as writers, learners, and thinkers. Turning to our data, we see agency coming into play in several ways:

- The student writer gains agency via the actions of instructors, who have created an opportunity for the meaningful writing project to take place.
- Agency is gained/performed by actors (both people and things) other than the instructor in relation to the meaningful writing project: classmates or peers, content/topic, and the meaningful writing project itself might all play agentive roles.
- Students imagine the meaningful writing project will help them gain agency in future writing situations.

In the following sections, we explore each of these topics, drawing on survey and interview data.

GAINING AGENCY THROUGH INSTRUCTORS AND THE MEANINGFUL WRITING PROJECT

When students offered reasons for why they chose a particular writing project as most meaningful, it was uncommon for them to note the role of their teacher. Interactions with the instructor of the course, which we coded *engagement*, occurred in only 7 percent of all survey responses (and *engagement* in our coding could also include interacting with individuals outside the classroom; responses that indicated working with peers or classmates we coded *collaboration*). Nevertheless, in our analysis of student-survey results, we saw a clear pattern emerge in terms of how particular writing assignments—and often the acts of faculty to shape and deliver those assignments—resulted in students' making note of a particular kind of agency. More specifically, in 31 percent of responses as to why they chose a project as meaningful, we heard seniors make some mention that it was because the project *allowed* or gave them the opportunity to pursue a topic or write in a particular form. At times, students were referring to the task itself—and thus tied it to the instructor in a somewhat indirect way—but other students specifically cited the instructor as the actor who "allowed" or "gave an opportunity":

- The professor gave us a lot of freedom in what topic to choose and how to explore it.
- Research project during my required writing course where the professor let us choose a topic of our liking.
- Writing is really a personal experience so the fact that the professor acted as a guide rather than a dictator really facilitated my improvement throughout the class.

In interviews, students offered more thorough accounts of the roles their instructors played, as in the following sociology major's account, which describes recognition of the professor's socially constructed learning context and how that led this student to take agency in rela-tion to her writing:

> She was very articulate, so a lot of the students respected her, but she was also very friendly and not really "I know more than you do." It was more "We're all learning together." She was always available. I could e-mail her my paper and ask her to look over it, make suggestions. I went to her office hours. I guess providing all of those activities and mixing it up because people have different learning styles, too, whether it's a self-review, or a peer review, or a group thing.

In another interview, a student responded this way to a question about the role her instructor played: "She acted as this guide. I don't know the role she played in other people's writing classes. I know for me it was very much why the project was meaningful. I think she played a role in that because she allowed us to make it meaningful for ourselves."

In survey responses, students made explicit reference to the role their instructors played in making the writing project meaningful:

- It was meaningful because I got to work closely with a faculty mentor on original research.
- I really enjoyed that I was able to work one on one with a teacher and that I was able to devote the entire semester to working on this project.
- It was the first time a professor went out of their way to make sure each student was writing something they were passionate about.
- The professor gave a lot of feedback throughout the process which facilitated the development of the project.

What is interesting is that every one of these responses describes some way in which the instructor's actions led to the students' development of their projects. Notice that students use words like "helped" and "facili-tated" in relation to implicitly or explicitly describing their own agency.

Much more frequently, however, students referred to their instructors indirectly through elements of the assignment in particular, emphasiz-ing the elements of choice or freedom we have already described, as in the following:

- I had great guidance and encouragement from my professor, but was given full flexibility in terms of what I focused on, how I approached my topic, how I did my research, etc.
- I was asked to construct an informational pamphlet, but was allowed a lot of creative freedom; we could choose the topic and even the medium in which the information was to be displayed.
- We were allowed to choose any topic we desire to write about in the field of medicine, science, etc.

- We were given the opportunity to choose a topic of interest to us and were guided through a writing process (emphasis on it as a process) to compose four polished documents each of a different genre.
- The essays were meaningful because I was given the opportunity to create my own research-based thesis, and explore a topic about which I am passionate.

Having been offered any degree of freedom to choose topics for their writing seemed particularly important for students to note, and their responses often spoke to how relatively rare it was for students to exercise this level of agency:

- I was able to pick a topic that speaks to me related to government on a personal level as opposed to working toward the professor's topical expectations.
- I actually could get to choose what I wanted to read and research about.
- In this paper I was finally able to choose my topic and research something I was very interested in.
- Normally, I don't have the opportunity to write about a topic I'm interested in.

Still, there was a clear limit to this freedom for many students, as an equally frequent pattern (occurring in 35 percent of all survey responses) was for students to remark that an instructor or writing task "required" or "forced" them into some action. And, at times, these qualities were almost symbiotic (emphasis added):

- This project was really useful because it *allowed* me to research something in my field academically and thoroughly. I was *forced* to find multiple valid sources, and from it, write something that was "real."
- I was *required* to come up with an original research question and create a grant proposal. . . . The project was meaningful because it *allowed* me to explore my creative scientific thinking.
- The project was so meaningful to me because it *allowed* me and *forced* me to relive moments I tried to forget and feelings I forgot I had.

Perhaps the ultimate sweet spot is found between instructor requirements and students' freedom to choose:

The paper itself was a research paper on a topic that we got to choose. I liked the fact that we got to discuss something we truly enjoyed from the class, and that the professor also had a narrow enough prompt to where we weren't floundering around for topic ideas. It gave us guidance without boundaries.

The contrast between "guidance" and "boundaries" appears significant to these writers as well. Too little of the former, and students are "floundering"; too many of the latter, and students are denied the agency to explore meaningful topics.

GAINING AGENCY THROUGH PEERS, CONTENT, TOPICS, AND THE MEANINGFUL WRITING PROJECT ITSELF

As we noted previously, when students mentioned in the survey an instructor, classmate, or peer as contributing to the meaningful writing project, we coded that response *engagement*. We were somewhat surprised surprised that *engagement* occurred in only 7 percent of all survey responses, given what we assumed to be the relatively common practice of peer review. However, in response to one of the National Survey of Student Engagement (NSSE) writing questions (which we describe in more detail in the next chapter), over 57 percent of students reported that they talked with "classmates, friends, or family members" before drafting, and nearly half received feedback from these noninstructor actors. In response to our survey question "Why meaningful?," students described peers and classmates as playing strong roles:

- I was able to choose topics that I found relevant to me and was able to give and receive feedback about my project from my peers.
- I was able to work with other students and create something that made me closer to my campus and could offer the same furthering bond to other people.
- I also loved how the class focused on writing instead of literary content—the writing process was different for this paper, because we went over drafts in class, did peer editing, and shared our final results with each other. In most English classes, you write the paper by yourself, hand it in, and wait for your final grade. This writing experience was much more engaging.

In addition to instructors and classmates, other actors in students' lives played strong roles in making their writing projects meaningful and, thus, helping them gain a sense of agency. One actor students described in the survey was the community in various forms, whether inside or outside the classroom:

- Being able to present my research and discuss it with major state political and educational figures made the project and its findings seem even more pressing and made the project resound even deeper with me.
- What made the project meaningful was that it allowed me to volunteer at a food shelter in Jamaica. It was nice to help others and do something meaningful.

- I volunteered with a private, tuition free elementary school for homeless children.
- When I know that my work will shed light on a subject or improve the design of something, I feel gratified. I am motivated to complete a writing project when I know it really help people and isn't purely academic.
- I felt this project was meaningful because I got to do real research to apply what I had learned in class. It also allowed me to get to know an elderly person. The experience overall was fantastic.

In addition to students' gaining a sense of agency through their actions of working with community members, we also saw that the content of students' projects themselves—and students' interaction with that content—led to a type of agency. As we note in chapter 1, the three most frequent codes for why students noted a writing project as meaningful were *personal connection, app+,* and *content learning.* In many of these instances, students made meaning through the interaction of these three elements. In other words, students had or made a connection to the content of the project itself, which, in turn, mapped onto students' sense of their past, present, and future lives. This identity-making in progress was thus enabled by the meaningful writing project:

- I truly cared about the content of the paper. I was exposed to the idea of it by some of my friends who are gay and researching more and more about it, I really loved the comparisons that I could draw between networks. I think another reason it was meaningful was knowing that the issue was real-life and something I could certainly see myself doing in a profession of my choosing.
- First of all, this paper was to be on a topic of my choosing, and I created this one, which makes it more personal and exciting from the start. But also, I believe that, much like in the era of the Depression, we are at a crossroads that requires a fundamental shift in how we think about national success. Subjective indicators are being adapted for Western use all the time, and the UN just endorsed the movement away from GDP alone in favor of a more comprehensive and subjective measurement of capability and prosperity. So, this topic is immediately relevant both to me and to the Western world.

What we see in these responses is the development of students' agency through their interaction with subject matter they truly care about or to which they have a personal (including career) connection. As one student described in an interview, "This [project] was the most meaningful because it was based on my own research rather than stuff I had found in books or online. I actually got to see firsthand what I was writing about."

MEANINGFUL WRITING AND FUTURE AGENCY

While agency is often activated within varied scenes of undergraduate writing—as students work from what Hull and Katz (2006) call "present capabilities"—we also observed a kind of agency that stretched toward "imagined futures," the places students could see themselves writing (44). More specifically, nearly 70 percent of all students surveyed felt their meaningful writing projects would be the type of writing they might encounter in the future. That the meaningful writing project they told us about often included this prescience suggests to us that fostering agency requires us to consider both *for now* and *for later*. Strauss and Xiang (2006) describe agency as demonstrated through "an awareness of the task at hand [and] an understanding of the demands of that task" (356). In one of our interviews, a student recognized the task, what was demanding about it, and how it would impact his future:

> It was meaningful because I was picturing myself like a professional. Those are the kinds of project reports that your boss could ask you to rewrite. I took this very seriously. It was meaningful because it was something new. But at the same time it was very, very demanding and then difficult at times. You need to gather your resources and then you need to have the adequate level of writing English skill.

We often saw students locating their future selves in relation to writing and imagining a kind of agency they would have in these situations:

- As a graduate school student I will have to discuss the theory behind my work in depth. As a career artist I also must be able to write about my work when I submit it to juried exhibitions.
- As a physician assistant I will have to write referral letters to other physicians, physician assistants, and health professionals to detail them about the status of our mutual patients. This is a particular writing skill that is vital for me to master and I felt that this writing project allowed me to mentally prepare myself for this important professional writing.
- As a teacher, I must write lesson plans that are creative—this project helped me to think outside the box.
- As an engineer I will be asked to write proposals for projects, memos about projects, and completion reports.
- As an environmental sciences major, it's important to be able to write clearly and concisely about the problems we tackle, but also to find the solutions that will benefit not just the victims, but also the perpetrators in order to best change their behavior.

We note here the intertwined nature of identity, writing, and subject matter and the ways these elements combine for students to imagine future agency. We must also note the complexity of writing tasks that are "practical" or keyed specifically to the kinds of writing students might do after graduation. On the one hand, we acknowledge the moving target students' futures provide and the dangers of narrowly constructing writing tasks with some sort of future in mind (as well as how difficult it is to convince students that a current writing task will be useful in some vague future context). On the other hand, we consistently see students in our study making those connections to their future selves, and their connections are not narrowly constructed. In other words, when they told us how they anticipated the future connections to their meaningful writing project experiences, students offered a fairly capacious view of how their meaningful writing projects would map to future writing situations.

- This type of project has given me confidence to pursue a masters degree.
- Yes! So much so. I want to take my analytic abilities elsewhere and apply them in the world! It really has given me the tool to take my skills other places.
- I would like to do the kinds of analysis used in this paper.
- Business writing is useful everywhere.

Whether these kinds of projects are the norm in our students' lives is a question we cannot answer; however, we are greatly encouraged by these possibilities for writing and its role in students' futures and their continued development of agency.

Of course, not all students felt their meaningful writing projects would connect to their future lives. As we noted previously, 31 percent of survey respondents cited a writing project as meaningful but responded "no" to "For the project you've described as meaningful, are there ways in which this writing project might contribute to the kinds of writing you hope to do in the future?" Students' responses to why they answered no to this question offer, in many cases, an imagined (or hoped for?) future without much writing:

- I am a business major so I don't see myself really using this writing in the future.
- I am going into a field that does not require a lot of writing.
- I do not intend on writing any technical papers in the future.
- I don't want to be a writer and hopefully won't have to write papers.

While we suspect that these students will encounter more writing in their futures than they anticipated as graduating seniors, these responses are most interesting when read against those students who *do* imagine their meaningful writing projects mapping onto future writing contexts. In many of those instances, students thought broadly about the skills, strategies, and habits of mind the meaningful writing project developed and invoked. They saw a role for writing in their futures that was far more than a certain type of task but was instead a way of connecting with subject matter, colleagues, and careers. As we describe in chapter 4, "Learning for Transfer," we think this phenomenon may also have something to do with how many of the opportunities created by meaningful writing projects were also opportunities in which learning was expansively framed (Engle et al. 2012).

THE ABSENCE OF AGENCY

As we noted earlier in this chapter, twenty-eight students filled out the entirety of our survey only to tell us they had not had any meaningful writing experiences. One way to understand these responses is to see them as the absence of agency. In fact, students often indicated that they felt they were missing out on what would have been a vital experience. As one student wrote,

> I don't remember any meaningful project because writing to me is more of a chore for me and I do not find it enjoyable, no matter what the topic. I usually feel that when I am writing for an assignment I am writing for a purpose that is not for myself, I am writing to appease the teacher and I am writing to get an "A."

We hoped, of course, that these students represented a small-but-vocal contingent, but we have no way of knowing for sure. And, of course, in light of Melzer's (2014) findings of the domination of "knowledge-telling" writing tasks, largely under timed, high-stakes conditions with the examiner as the only audience, the opportunities for meaningful writing—and, thus, agency—might not be as widespread as we would hope. As Melzer (2014) states in the conclusion to his study, "Sixty-six percent of the assignments had informative purposes, with an emphasis on informing the reader (almost always the expert instructor) about factual details from a lecture or readings" (104). Consider one student who compared the meaningful writing project experience to all of her other writing projects (which she might as well have characterized as *not meaningful*):

> It contributed to my ability to enjoy writing papers. I like writing papers that can have a degree of creativity and even humor in them (even though the opportunities are few and far between in college), and writing papers like that periodically helps me write better when I am writing the

comparatively dull stuff. It's easier to color within the lines the rest of the time if every so often you get a chance to scribble all over the page; if that metaphor makes sense.

What is most interesting to us about the responses from the "no-meaningful-writing" group is that the absences they make note of are in accord with the themes we saw for those who did have meaningful writing projects; in other words, they note the need for personal connection, for content learning, for applicability and relevance and, in several cases, for creativity and choice. They recognize what the assignment was "not" (Nowacek 2011) but remain unable to articulate what it *could be.*

We did also wonder whether this set of twenty-eight students was somehow different demographically from the group as a whole. As shown in figure 2.1, this group's profile largely fit the profile of all survey respondents, representing disciplines from accounting to zoology, so we cannot conclude that particular majors might result in a lack of meaningful writing experiences. And these students were pretty much evenly distributed across our three institutions, ruling out institutional differences as a factor.

Some of this group, like the student quoted above, seemed simply to not identify as writers:

- I don't really like writing.
- I hate writing.
- I do not plan on writing for my career.
- I'm not a fan of writing.

Most of the other students expressed disappointment that the writing they had encountered did not offer opportunities for agency. For several students, even the genre-based writing connected to their chosen fields was far from meaningful:

- I can be honest and say that I haven't one writing project during my undergraduate career meaningful. As a science major I have been delegated to writing lab reports and research proposals almost exclusively. There have been no opportunities to write opinionated, personal pieces or works of fiction.
- Did not have any writing projects that were meaningful because I did not have to take English because of AP credits and the rest were pertaining to lab reports (not meaningful).
- Writing project in business school? no.

For some, the writing they encountered simply did not inspire them or create much excitement:

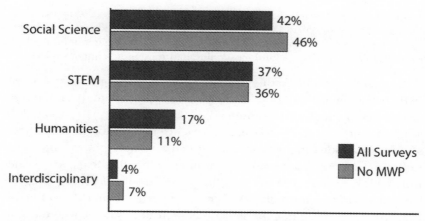

Figure 2.1. Majors of all survey respondents compared to those who indicated no meaningful writing projects.

- I didn't really have any meaningful writing projects; they all seemed uninspired and the prompts weren't unique.
- I did not find the writing to be anything fantastic. It was all very bland and did not incorporate much creativity.
- I would have found a writing project that allowed me to express my creativity or one that allowed me to project my ideas and opinions to be meaningful.

For others, the lack of personal connection and relevance to their lives and careers meant an absence of meaningful writing:

- I cannot remember any writing projects that I have had. So, I believe it is a safe assumption that none of the writing projects I had had a great impact on me.
- Any writing I've completed for [my university] has been academically driven and graciously assessed. While they may have promoted some analytical thought at times, the types of writing that I have been asked to complete have no bearing on my future professional endeavors.
- The writing that is done in college does not apply to real life. I do not use any type of writing, that is part of my college courses, in my professional career. The professional career people I come in contact with do not write in any manner they did in college. I teach adults, and I don't write in the manner that is dictated in college.

For one student, meaningful education needed to be self-sponsored or completed independently:

None of my writing projects have really stood out to me. My hope was to become a sports writer, but found no outlet or classes that catered to that desire. Instead I was lumped in with the rest of the [journalism college's] students and shoveled the same thing that everyone is. . . . I understand that its part of the curriculum to make the students balanced and to, in theory, be on the same page. This was boring and left me feeling unfulfilled. My greatest experiences (and most enjoyable) were independent projects.

Ultimately, students in this group did not find writing to matter much in their academic lives. Some strongly wished that had not been the case or that writing might have promoted the kind of agency they seemed to yearn for and expect their college experience to produce. Instead, these seniors are graduating without having had a meaningful writing experience, an absence that seems unfortunately familiar (e.g., Arum and Roksa 2011) and is a reminder of the powerful role of writing as agentive—at least for some students. The Meaningful Writing Project helps reveal the difference in experiences between the students who did not find agency through writing and the students who did.

CASE STUDIES OF MEANINGFUL WRITING AND AGENCY

In the case studies that follow, we explore students' development of agency in more depth, beginning with a student who was largely an exception to our overall trends: her meaningful writing project did not take place in a class context, yet it helped her develop a sense of agency over her writing in contrast to what she had experienced in school-based tasks. Our second case study features a student in a business-ethics class finding his way as a writer who wants to balance creativity with how he might have an influence in the professional discourse in his field. In both cases, agency is enabled by interaction with others (whether faculty or family members), with experiences and topics, and with students' hoped-for futures.

CASE STUDY 1—LEAH: AGENCY AND A FAMILY AUDIENCE

Our first case study of student agency via a meaningful writing project focuses on Leah,[2] a senior physical therapy major, who identified on our survey as a "White/Caucasian," "female," and "22–25 years old." Leah described her meaningful writing project as follows: "After my trip to China, I wrote an article about it and my experiences working in a pediatric burn unit." When responding to the question of why this project was meaningful, Leah wrote, "I got to explain the trip in my own way and be creative. I also got to put pictures in of my trip." We coded this

---

[2] In this first case study and in all other uses of student and faculty names in this book, we have created pseudonyms to ensure participant confidentiality.

response *creative* and *personal connection.* Leah also indicated she had not written anything like this article previously and did not imagine doing this type of writing in her future, noting, "My future career will be physical therapy where I'll be writing a lot of patient notes but nothing more than that unless I get into research."

In Leah's interview with Pedro, a senior English major, she reveals an uncertain history with writing and how this family-oriented out-of-school task brought to bear her interests and experiences. The agency she experienced with this meaningful writing project might not necessarily have turned her from a reluctant writer to an eager one or mapped onto the future writing she might do as a physical therapist, but in the moment it gave her a certain power over her experiences and a way to convey those experiences to a real audience. In other words, it was a meaningful writing opportunity Leah contrasted with her previous writing opportunities.

In terms of her history as a writer, Leah tells Pedro, "I'm not a good writer. . . . I get very frustrated with writing, and I hit a block. . . . I think I chose a path to avoid reading and writing since they're my weaknesses." When she describes the writing she has done as an undergraduate, she reveals more uncertainty and unease:

> I'm a physical therapy major, so we don't really have to write much. We had, I think, our sophomore writing class. I don't even remember. Then our advanced writing class. I think we had two writing classes in all. I wouldn't say it helped or hurt me in either way. I'm pretty neutral about them. One was more research based, I'd say, and neutral. They didn't do much. They frustrated me because I'm not good at writing.

When Leah talks more specifically about the kind of writing she's done as an undergraduate, she refers several times to her feelings of a forced march of sorts with a predetermined structure. She expresses a wish that the writing assignments would have been more creative and allowed more freedom or agency:

> If [the writing] was more of an open, free write, I think it would have helped. Because then I feel like my mind could have taken me to, "Oh, well this is where my mind's thinking, so I want to write about that," as opposed to, "This is where they're forcing my mind to go, and I don't know what to write about, and this is the structure of the project, but I'm not passionate about it so it's harder to write about."

In contrast to these school-based tasks, the writing Leah did for her family newsletter allowed her to connect to a passion and to be creative. Here's how she describes the project to Pedro:

I went on a trip to China to work at a pediatric burn unit in Beijing. We have a big family, and so we have a family newsletter that goes out four times a year. I was asked to write an article about the trip to China in the newsletter. Basically, it was just free writing and just explaining what I learned, funny instances, what I saw, what a typical day was, stuff like that.

For Leah, her newsletter article had a specific, familiar audience: her family members. And her "literacy sponsor" (Brandt 1998) in this case was a cousin who was the editor of the newsletter and who gave her feedback on her initial draft. Still, while the task had exigency for Leah, her processes for creating the newsletter article weren't without struggle. As she describes, "I was stuck for a good hour. I just kept thinking, 'Oh, I don't know what to write, I don't know how to start this.'" Eventually, she chose to start, "writing it like a letter home, to family, or journal entry almost, and that's when it came out easier."

Ultimately, then, Leah was able to capture in writing her experience as an unpaid volunteer with an organization that helps pediatric burn patients with medical care. Her experiential learning seems particularly relevant here, which she contrasts with the classroom-based learning in her past:

[The experience] was different because I didn't have to write about any research or any medical things, and I was learning all new stuff since I hadn't really learned anything about burns here. It was something new, and more that I didn't have to study or look up anything and write about somebody else's work, and I had all the knowledge to write it, and that I could just write. It wasn't that I had to find other knowledge and learn more to write it.

While Leah's reluctance to engage in library research in order to write—a common task in her required writing classes—is somewhat discouraging to those of us who assign and value such assignments, we do wonder whether it is possible to capture the qualities she valued and that gave her agency in this meaningful project in order to return them to classroom contexts. What she became knowledgeable about on the trip was appealing both because it was new and because it was learned experientially. The balance between *allow* and *require* once again seems key in Leah's experience, and we wonder whether her writing experiences up to this point were too close to the *require* end of the continuum with not enough *allow*. Her agency seems closely tied to the freedom and creativity she could bring to bear on this writing project. As she notes in her interview, "I think creativity is not my strong suit, so I feel like, with another project, if I couldn't have been creative, as maybe why I wouldn't like it as much as I did with this one." Leah also received tangible, positive feedback from her relatives once they read her article, which offered a sense of accomplishment and perhaps some shift in her self-identity as a writer with an audience: "When I got responses from people, it was great to know that people were actually reading it and that they appreciated it. They complimented me on my writing, which I always think is terrible, so it's good to hear that."

Near the end of their interview, Pedro asks Leah if there were any other significant takeaways from this meaningful writing project. Leah's response indicates the role she sees for writing as a way of making sense of her experiences:

> I think being able to reflect back on the trip was significant. Maybe when I was there I didn't realize what bothered me, what didn't, what I was learning, what I could have skipped. Reflecting back on it, I realized more of "This was a good experience, this was a bad experience. I would have changed this. I regret doing this."

Pedro follows up this response by asking if such reflection is a common practice for Leah. She responds, "I don't think I write enough to be able to reflect enough." In our hopeful moments we wonder whether the air of regret Leah expresses here would spur her on to engage in more reflective writing. Was the agency she experienced with her newsletter article—in control of not merely the processes of writing but also the opportunity to connect meaningful content to a real audience—a one-time occurrence? Leah does note to Pedro that she might write more for the family newsletter in the future, but she imagines a career largely devoid of such creative and open-ended writing experiences, those closely tied to *personal connection.* Of course, many other students we surveyed and interviewed were able to find creative space and personal connection with school-based tasks, perhaps even with the same kind of tasks Leah experienced. The spaces we create for students to experience agency are not always yet inhabited—but understanding (and creating) those spaces is a necessary, though not sufficient, condition for meaningful writing to occur.

CASE STUDY 2—ERIK: AGENCY AND A VISION OF A FUTURE SELF

Our second case study of student agency via a meaningful writing project is Erik, a senior finance major who identified in our survey as "Asian," "male," and "18–21." He described his meaningful writing project as follows: "Analyzing the impact of business ethics in today's economy and society." When we asked why his project was meaningful, Erik wrote, "The relevance to today's ethically volatile and corrupted business practices." We coded this response *app+*. Erik said he had never before written anything like this project when he took his class as a sophomore but that he did plan to write something like it in the future. In fact, he expressed a goal for himself in his survey response: "I intend to contribute to the journal of business ethics looking into privacy and social implications in the development of technology and business information systems."

In his interview, Erik had much more to say about the experience of writing his meaningful writing project; the role his instructor, who was adjunct faculty, played in supporting his writing and revision process; the relationship between thinking of himself as a creative writer and/ or a business writer; and the way in which this one project in a required business-ethics class showed him the agency that could be possible for him as a professional and scholarly voice in the field of business.

Erik tells his interviewer, an undergraduate writing center consultant, he felt his professor's passion and describes his professor's "strong interest in taking theoretical principles and applying them practically to issues of business development." His writing assignment, which occurred toward the end of the semester, was to take a major theme from the business-ethics book, look at articles from business leaders, and "go with it and argue." Erik set out to develop an argument against privacy and wanted to propose that privacy holds back business development. And he says he learned through the writing and revision process that the piece he was creating had to "provide change or raise topics that people don't normally think about and you need to have not only a strong argument but the facts behind it."

When the undergraduate interviewer asks Erik what he believes makes a writing project meaningful, he says, "What makes papers meaningful to me is the [professor's] ability to present a growth opportunity for a student." When the interviewer asks Erik what he means by "growth opportunity," Erik elaborates by explaining how a professor would say, "I'm not grading you on your ability to piece together sentences and ideas in an elementary sense. It's more presenting this is an opportunity for you to grow as a person, for you to grow as a writer." The interviewer asks him what the professor did or said in their meetings that helped him see this project through, and he says, "He saw my vision, he saw what I was capable of. He asked why? Why are you thinking that?" Erik says his professor worked to find out what he thought was truly important in all he was trying to argue, and he was "inquisitive to my thought process." And he says his professor "really wanted [him] to see this paper."

It's interesting to hear what Erik says about his sense of himself as a writer coming into the process of writing his meaningful writing project and then, later, as a senior, in reflection on what happened for him as he wrote the project:

> I'm a creative writer at heart, but when I stepped into business, as a student, I had to really adjust and grow in that type of environment. That forced me to be more concise and my writing to be more definitive in that aspect. That's what made me write this paper. I was just passionate at the time. I was so geared to prepare myself to write this paper. It was unbelievable how everything just matched up with my growing interests and just the overall subject matter.

In reflecting on his project, Erik clearly had a sense that his professor was aware of the knowledge (and perhaps passion) students might have and the knowledge—both writing knowledge and disciplinary and professional stance—they might need to learn from him. And Erik could tell not every student in his class was as open to this learning and to his professor's mentorship as he was:

> I think he was one of the professors that really took strides in taking students to a different level in terms of not only writing creatively but having facts behind your suggestions or being more a writer that was not only producing fluff and attractive pieces, the kind of things that are factual and can be put in journals. It gave me that idea. I never thought that it would be possible to produce writing like this, so that happened in the perfect timing, if you will. Some students obviously didn't take advantage, because I was really, really passionate about this piece, but that's basically it.

In Erik's mind, his professor had led students up to this project through earlier assignments: in "the other writing assignments, he stressed the structure and having proper syntax, just proper structure through your paper in general, and having a theme that linked everything together. That's what connected his assignments as well, was that constant push for having students really express their thoughts in a structured way that was argumentative, yet having substance."

Erik described meeting with his professor more than ten times during the semester—sometimes right after class and sometimes in the early morning in the adjunct lounge—but, as his interviewer described in a postinterview reflection, "Strangely, his writing process was a one nighter, which lasted 20 hours." The interview exchange that explains Erik's writing process and interaction with his professor is worth reproducing here. With a tone reminiscent of one of our favorite meaningful writing project survey quotes, in which a student says, "Though I cannot stand the professor or the majority of what she teaches . . . ,"

Erik notes that his professor's approach did not leave him happy, but it left him determined.

> *Robert:* How was the process? What process did you take in writing this?
>
> *Erik:* I paired up my ideas that I had with each article that was in the textbook and drew it out. It was probably one of the most well-planned pieces of mine. Just doing piece by piece by piece by piece, eventually connecting everything and having some type of synergy. That took a while.
>
> Then finally, him critiquing it in the adjunct office at like 8 a.m. when I pulled an all-nighter for the paper. Him telling me it's a lot of stuff there, boil it down to about five pages. Moving from twenty to five pages was a challenge. All of that together motivated me, pushed me. I didn't like him, to be honest, throughout the whole semester. I did not like him.
>
> The reason why I did not is because, looking back, he pushed me more than I wanted to be pushed. But looking back it helped me to develop as a business student and gaining a writing style that was not only influential but really had substance in it. Not just, like I said, I was more of a creative writer to begin with. Having thoughts and producing entertaining pieces or producing pieces that were analytical and thought provoking was my nature. But just pairing that style and that passion up with something that was so business centric, that was just an amazing journey to complete that.
>
> *Robert:* How did he push you?
>
> *Erik:* He definitely was not confrontational. He pushed me very indirectly by just saying, in a really structured way, "Narrow the piece down, use this as support. Your piece lacks substance. Your piece does not reflect this quality that you put in your introduction. It doesn't fully explain it properly." Just little things, and as the piece developed and grew, he was there to really provide guidelines for the structure of the piece.
>
> *Robert:* What was your immediate reaction when you walked out of the office hearing about all that?
>
> *Erik:* I had other finals at the time and I was crestfallen, because I thought that I had produced an incredible masterpiece that took twenty hours to do. At the end of the day I looked at myself and I said, "You know what? It's not about producing words." It's more about—not even attractive and just wonderful words—but just more has to have structure. It has to have structure. It has to have substance. It has to have these qualities that make it meaningful to a bigger audience, not only a selective group. Having a business paper, you need to provide change or you need to raise topics that people don't normally think of. To immediately challenge someone's viewpoint, you need to have not only a strong argument but also the facts behind it. That's what I understood from the piece.

As a senior, Erik feels that this project, and this mentorship, was key to who he became as a writer in college. He tells his interviewer, "He didn't add the structure. We did. That was incredible." And he goes on to say, "The ability to take the piece apart and analyze it and put it back together and see what was there and what was not there. I think that analytical piece and that businesslike characteristic of his critiques were really important. That's what translated across all my writing pieces until today."

Toward the end of their interview, the undergraduate interviewer pushes Erik to say a bit more about what professors can do to support meaningful writing experiences for students. He says, "Give everyone the benefit of the doubt that the whole room, everyone, is capable of writing an incredible piece that's going to impact the whole world." To us, that's a good description of teaching writing for student agency.

CONCLUSION

In the case of meaningful writing, students' development of agency is rooted in their interactions with texts, subject matter, teachers, peers, and family members, as well as with personal histories and future aspirations. Their acknowledgment of these relationships and the roles these relationships play looks like the kind of reflectiveness "special to human agency" (Bratman 2000, 61), particularly if students see the ultimate goal as the further development of agency via planning for their future selves. Like empowerment, agency is not something we can (or should) bestow on students. At best, we can intentionally build optimal conditions for agency to emerge. Agency is strengthened by offering experiences that get students to notice they have the capacity to direct energies for themselves, in and beyond classrooms.

Writing remains a key to entering a discourse community, and one might argue that those students who chose to identify a meaningful writing project and respond to our survey were those who found success in that endeavor. We cannot conclude that all others were not successful, of course, but we can draw from our research data to better understand the relationship among identity, discourse, and agency and, in particular, the interactions among students, instructors, and peers—and content—that make agency possible. And we saw that *personal connection* was a prominent feature in the meaningful writing projects. But the felt sense of the value and pleasure of the project was evidenced through other features as well, such as *choice*. One student remarked that the choice he had in both the direction and topic of his project was "the most rewarding part":

> If I ever do any research on my own in the future, it's going to have to be something that I'm going to have to like, want to be really interested in, to put all the time and effort into it. But also be able to build it from the ground up, and not be like just trying to meet some criteria of a professor . . . something that I'm going to have to gather all the information for

and be able to convince a third party person of my argument, rather than my professor, who knows what the right answer is. . . . That's why this one was probably the most valuable writing experience I had.

His recognition that future writing tasks will require *his* "time and effort to build it from the ground up" speaks of agency. Whether we call it *maturity, self-actualization, self-efficacy,* or *self-authorship* (Baxter Magolda 1999), any view of writers as developing (a view we three share) will agree that the conditions and opportunities designed within a writing assignment can contribute to further development of agency. As Juan Guerra (2015) explains, citing the New London Group's work, " It is not enough for students to articulate or critique what they have learned and now understand, that is, it is not enough for them to become aware in a self-reflective manner of their newly acquired knowledge; they must also be able to engage in transformed practice: teachers must give students actionable opportunities 'to demonstrate how they can design and carry out, in a reflective manner, new practices embedded in their own goals and values'" (110). Helping students realize agency—as they gain control of their academic, intellectual, and professional present lives and ever-expanding futures—is a goal we can all easily support.

3
ENGAGEMENT AND THE MEANINGFUL WRITING PROJECT

A project that comes to mind was my first essay I had to write for college. It was for my History class (1865 to Present) and the topic was project MKULTRA, a covert domestic operation by the CIA that included the use of human subjects to develop methods of mind control. I can't remember the thesis exactly, but the goal of the assignment was for students to get an idea of how argumentative writing should be done and why including good sources in a paper is critical as well as the sourcing itself. Students were to use at least 10 primary sources and 10 secondary sources and include a works cited page.

I found this to be really significant for my college career for several reasons:

It was my first college paper, and so I really wanted to do well on it.

My argumentative writing was already good from high school, but this paper helped me A LOT with my sourcing skills. I can honestly say that if I didn't have this assignment at the time I did, the rest of my writing in my college career would not have been as good as it was.

It helped me appreciate college professors, the writing center, and critiquing in general. While I was writing I was given great feedback on my paper, that helped me end up with a great finished product and a good grade.

—Psychology major

While students' development of agency, the subject of our previous chapter, is a key outcome of meaningful writing projects, evidence of engagement seems a priori to these projects—it would be impossible to label something meaningful without having engaged with it. At the risk of simplifying a complex process, agency can be seen as an outcome of sorts, while engagement is a process that often leads to that outcome, and in this chapter we explore that process in depth. Still, engagement is by no means a given—the components required to provide opportunities for engagement cannot be taken for granted. Current research suggests access to engagement is regulated for some students by low academic self-concept, stereotype threat, preparedness, gender,

DOI: 10.7330/9781607325802.c003

race, parental support, and other invisible factors (Bundick et al. 2014, 10–11). We recognize that not all students find themselves invited to engage, and not all actors believe they have a responsibility to engage/ be engaged beyond providing perfunctory instruction or regurgitating content. Recall that twenty-eight students in this study did not experience a meaningful writing project, going out of their way to tell us they were not engaged with teachers or topics. However, for the great majority of students in this study, meaningful writing projects provided an opportunity to engage with instructors, peers, and community members, as well as with the content and processes of their writing and learning.

Of course, we are not saying that their meaningful writing projects were students' only opportunity to be plugged into their educations, but the relationship between writing and student engagement has been clearly recognized. In his study of undergraduates, Light (2004) found that

> the relationship between the amount of writing for a course and students' level of engagement—whether engagement is measured by time spent on the course, or the intellectual challenge it presents, or students' level of interest in it—is stronger than the relationship between students' engagement and any other course characteristic. It is stronger than the relation between students' engagement and their impressions of their professor. It is far stronger than the relationship between level of engagement and *why* a student takes a course (required versus elective; major field versus not in the major field). The simple correlation between the amount of writing required in a course and students' overall commitment to it tells a lot about the importance of writing. (55–56)

Light's definition of engagement—essentially following Kuh (2009) and others in looking at "the time and effort students devote to activities that are empirically linked to desired outcomes of college *and* what institutions do to induce students to participate in these activities" (683)—represent one dimension of what we saw happening in students' accounts of their meaningful writing projects. But another dimension of what we heard from the seniors in our study, included in the example with which we opened this chapter, demonstrates that engagement is a social process. In this chapter we describe the three primary ways we saw engagement socially enacted: with instructors and peers, with learners' future selves, and with nonhuman entities, such as course content or writing processes. These findings are mirrored in those of other researchers: Matthew Bundick et al. (2014) confirm that "student engagement is highly likely to arise in classrooms where student-teacher relationships are strong, students perceive content to be relevant, and they perceive the teacher to be an expert in the content and effective at delivering it" (17). It seems then that the responsibility for engagement does not reside only in the student, only in the teacher, or only in the content. Engagement may be a requisite part of the process of learning and teaching writing, as it enriches the opportunities to bring writers, purposes, and content together, and as we show in this study, that point of intersection is often a student's meaningful writing project.

The survey response we offer at the beginning of this chapter also reveals how this student's feeling of accomplishment, experiences with writing to learn (in this case, focused on citation and documentation), and engagement with his professor and the writing center led to even greater and more wide-ranging engagement, as well as to a sense of agency (chapter 2) and a certainty that he had learned for transfer (chapter 4). This student had done similar writing before. As he told us in his survey answer, "For my senior year in high school, we had this assignment called an Extended Essay, a 4000-word paper required by the IB program (sort of like AP, but not really) I was enrolled in. It was an argumentative paper as well and sources were required." But in his first year of college, his professor's goal "for students to get an idea of how argumentative writing should be done and why including good sources in a paper is critical as well as the sourcing itself" led to a belief in himself and in his researching and writing skills. As he wrote, "I can honestly say that if I didn't have this assignment at the time I did, the rest of my writing in my college career would not have been as good as it was." When he reflected, as a senior, all the way back on this writing experience from his first year of college, he could see and name the way engagement and accomplishment led to further accomplishment. But would he have been as motivated as a first-year student if the topic hadn't been so interesting (he could remember MKULTRA even though he couldn't remember the argument he made about it)? Would he have sustained his motivation without engagement with others who wanted to help him reach the accomplishment he craved?

As we consider the relationship between engagement and students' most meaningful writing projects, this student's account strikes us as a kind of engagement we saw repeatedly in our survey and interview results: new writing tasks or new ways of writing or new depths of learning (that certainly could have built on previous experiences) combined for students with an investigation of a topic or participation in a process that offered interest or personal connection (and, thus, motivation) and engagement with others—a professor, peers, writing center consultants.

The result represented meaningful opportunities in which the students were engaged with their learning and their writing.

In this chapter, we explore this social view of engagement and also consider ideas about engagement that come from the National Survey of Student Engagement (NSSE), as well as published findings from the Consortium for the Study of Writing in College, a partnership between NSSE and the Council of Writing Program Administrators, in response to NSSE Topical Module: Experiences with Writing. In our student survey, we included three sets of NSSE writing questions, allowing us to compare our results with national NSSE results from 2012, the same year we collected student data for the Meaningful Writing Project. In this chapter, we include students' comments from the open-ended portion of those questions, adding depth to the check-box results inherent in the NSSE questions alone.

ENGAGEMENT AS A SOCIAL PROCESS

As we noted at the start of this chapter, viewing engagement as an individual's "sense of investment and involvement in learning" (5), as the *Framework for Success in Post-Secondary Writing* (CWPA, NCTE, and NWP 2011) describes it (where engagement is one of the "habits of mind" to be developed by a learner), neglects the social role of engagement or the instances in which engagement is a social process. This reframing from the individual to the social is consistent with the overall trend toward social theories of learning and helps us understand how individual writers are shaped, and in turn shape, the practices of the discourse communities in which they are situated (e.g., Bazerman 1994; Gee 2004; Miller 1984; Wenger 1999).

In fact, a socioecological view seems to be emerging that sees engagement "as the conceptual glue that connects student agency (including students' prior knowledge, experience, and interests) and its ecological influences (peers, family and community) to the structures and cultures of school" (Lawson and Lawson 2013, 433). Retaining this view pushes back on critiques of measuring engagement for neoliberal ends. The NSSE is not without its detractors, as it continues to provide data to support "an audit culture" that views learning as "performing in certain ways to achieve specified outcomes" (Zepke 2014, 701). Our view of student writing experiences, however, is influenced by student voices as they tell us how their meaningful writing projects were underwritten, so to speak, by a professor, friend, or family member or by the content and processes of the project itself.

In our coding of "Why meaningful?," as well as in students' open-ended responses following the NSSE writing questions on our survey, we saw consistent patterns of engagement as a social process. Most prominently, we saw descriptions of interactions with instructors and peers as types of engagement around and with meaningful writing projects. We also saw students describing interactions with future selves or future communities, particularly as they imagined the meaningful writing project as the kind of writing they might do postgraduation. Finally, we saw many examples of students engaging with the content of their meaningful writing projects, as well as with the writing and research processes they used to compose those projects. We next offer examples of each of these types of social engagement.

ENGAGEMENT WITH OTHERS—INSTRUCTORS, PEERS AND AUDIENCES

As we noted in the previous chapter, in students' "Why meaningful?" survey responses, we coded a response as *engagement* when it invoked an interaction with an instructor or peer as contributing to the meaningfulness of the project. This code occurred in 7 percent of all survey responses—thus, not particularly frequently. However, students' responses to the NSSE writing questions do offer additional evidence that instructors and peers played a strong role for many, as we will describe in the second half of this chapter.

Student responses recalled faculty support, attention, and competence as factors contributing to a meaningful writing project. For example, "Why meaningful?" responses often invoked engagement with instructors in terms of support and guidance:

- I really enjoyed that I was able to work one on one with a teacher.
- I had an excellent instructor who helped make the research project come alive for me.
- The topic was interesting and the professor took an interest in each student's work.
- I had great guidance and encouragement from my professor.

Since we also offered students the opportunity to add additional comments to two of the sets of NSSE writing questions—"the kind of writing you did" and "the process you used to write" the meaningful writing project—we also heard students describing engagement in their responses to those questions. It's worth noting that we did not offer the opportunity to write open-ended responses for the set of questions on "the role of your instructor" (an oversight on our part!); nevertheless, students frequently described engagement with their instructor in their extended responses to the NSSE questions, without prompting:

- I only wish I had time to take more classes with Professor W___. She changed how I think about writing and creating.
- The project I chose to do was very complex—the ideas that I wanted to express could not be resolved quickly or easily. But my Professor remained available to answer my questions as and when I came up with them, and pushed me to probe even deeper into issues that I had only scratched on the surface.
- This was the best class and professor that I ever had. Not only was the information clear, interesting, and fun, but the teacher was as well. It is always such a better experience when the professor actually enjoys being there and teaching.

Consistent with what we describe in chapter 2 about the balance between required elements and student freedom to explore and learn, many of these responses also described the role of the instructor to offer this kind of support along with ample freedom:

- We were given lab reports, but clear instructions were not given because the point of the labs were to figure it out yourself. The professor was there for guidance.
- He gave you freedom to choose the topic as it related to the course.
- Prof said this is your paper, you decide everything.

Still, for one survey respondent, engagement with the instructor was not dependent on a carefully cultivated relationship but on the opportunity the assignment created: "Though I cannot stand the professor or the majority of what she teaches, her open-ended term paper allowed me to really explore my own theory on films and apply that to a really good term paper."

While engagement with instructors was noted in survey responses, we also saw engagement with peers as contributing to the meaningful writing projects, particularly in the use of structured peer review though also in terms of discussion with and presentation to peers:

- My professor made us read our papers in class so that it was open for critique. Although this was nerve-wracking especially since it was my first semester ever, it was a good experience for public speaking and to get great feedback from my Professor and my classmates.
- We were forced to self-edit and read others' works for feedback. It forced me to look at my own writing in a different way and forced me to be critical in an effective way towards other peoples' writings.

- This project was meaningful because it was largely student driven. Students are allowed to write about something they are passionate about and really solidify their knowledge of a specific content area. They are then encouraged to share their discoveries and research with their peers.
- The presentation of our papers sparked a lot of interesting comments from my classmates as each gave their own interpretation of the Scripture based on their individual religious backgrounds.

Still, not all students expressed satisfaction with the peer-review process. One student's response following the NSSE writing questions captures this perspective:

> I hate peer review and I'm glad I've only had to do it a handful of times. It's misleading and a waste of time to pretend that students are writing for anyone other than their professors. Unless the person reviewing your paper is a significantly better writer than you are, their comments are pretty much useless, since what they think of your writing means nothing if your professor doesn't agree.

Given that this was the only negative comment we saw in regard to peer review in over seven hundred survey responses, we can consider it an outlier. Still, the kinds of engagement schooling structures *and* values, particularly when grades are attached to writing projects and students are writing only for the professor (Melzer 2014), might make the lack of such responses more surprising.

Another way we saw engagement with peers mentioned in our survey data occurred in "Why meaningful?" responses we coded *collaboration*; these specifically named working in groups or with others as contributing to the meaningful writing project:

- It showed me that I worked well in an online team setting that required multiple parts and significant participation.
- I was able to work with other students and create something that made me closer to my campus and could offer the same furthering bond to other people.
- Because the assignment was to be completed as a group it required us to work together to write and edit the memo. We had to project the paper onto a screen and then discuss collectively how to improve the writing and edit the paper most effectively.
- It was a group collaboration that involved team work and effort, which all paid off in the end.
- I was able to work with groups. I had lot of interaction with classmates.

We need to note that the code *collaboration* occurred only ten times, or roughly in 1 percent of all survey responses (though as indicated in responses to the NSSE writing questions as shown in fig. 3.3, 18 percent of our survey respondents reported that their meaningful writing projects were part of group projects). Perhaps this finding reveals the lack of collaborative work offered in many classes or that the process of collaboration might not be what leads to a meaningful writing project. With our limited data, we can only speculate.

ENGAGEMENT WITH FUTURE SELVES

Another kind of social engagement we saw repeatedly in our data was interaction (experienced and anticipated) with future selves, future colleagues, and future professions. Both in the "Why meaningful?" responses we coded as *app+* and in students' responses to how their meaningful writing project would be similar to the kind of writing they would do in the future, we saw many responses situated within students' imagined professional careers, including the communication tasks they believed they would be experiencing and the kinds of content they would encounter:

- It was meaningful because it actually gave me a chance to think about my plans for the future. It got me thinking of what I want to do and how I would get to where I want to be.
- It allowed me to learn how to create and interpret discourse between professionals in my field; I got to hone my skills in writing within my future profession, not just how to structure an essay or a research paper.
- The project was meaningful to me because I am studying to become a Physician Assistant so the research interested me and my findings directly applied to my future.
- The writing assignment assisted in evaluating myself and students of all disabilities on the classroom. As a future educator the research is very helpful and eye opening.
- Anti-human trafficking is an important issue to me, so being able to write a report that allowed me to explore the issue more was very meaningful. Writing became more exciting because I was extremely interested in the topic and it pertained to my future.

The final example reveals how engagement may develop from the ways in which *personal connection* to the issue brings the student to the topic and then carries the student's thinking to a future, one in which, as she told us in her survey response, she imagined she "might write research reports or specific plans for NGO's in the anti-trafficking field."

For those who responded "yes" to our survey question "For the project you've described as meaningful, are there ways in which this writing project might contribute to the kinds of writing you hope to do in the future?," invoking that specific career role was common:

- One of my future aspirations is to become a novelist, and thus pursuing and completing this project has brought me one step closer to achieving my goals.

- I plan on being an elementary school teacher and I believe that rich, detailed writings will always be beneficial.

- I will continue to write these documents so long as I am employed as a Software/Web Developer.

- I hope to take the skills that I honed during this project and carry them forward as a design engineer with strong written communication skills.

- It is quite likely that in my career as a scientist, I will constantly be writing grants in order to gain funding for various research endeavors. I am glad to be learning how to write a proper grant, especially in an academic environment where my work can be reviewed and critiqued without real grant money on the line.

In these instances, we see a kind of mutual engagement with future selves centered on the writing students expect to do (or a type of learning for transfer we explore in the next chapter). The meaningful writing project connects the present to these futures, often tying to the success students imagine they will experience given what they now know. Thus, engagement and identity are intertwined.

ENGAGEMENT WITH CONTENT AND PROCESSES

An important kind of engagement we saw occurring in our data was not necessarily with other people but with other *things*, namely the content of students' writing, the processes they used to complete their projects, and the projects themselves. In terms of the last, when we asked for additional comments following our NSSE writing questions, several students offered the ways their meaningful writing project figured into subsequent presentation or publication, extending their engagement with content and processes beyond the context that prompted it, and, in many cases, beyond campus:

- I have presented this research paper and project at 3 different research conferences.

- I presented my research at Eastern Sociology Society Conference in 2012.

- I presented my research on 3/31 at Tufts' Future of Food and Nutrition Conference.

- I submitted my paper to the English department's Hanson Writing Competition last year, and was honored to win first place for scholarly writing.

- My instructor asked to use a portion of my paper for a book he was writing.

- This report was 182 pages; it was also used to submit work to file for a provisional patent application.

- I have submitted my final paper to 1 collection of student work and am currently revising the paper to submit it to a student journal.

Undergraduate research, in all the forms described by these quotes, is designated a "high-impact practice" by the AACU, and, as Kuh notes, engagement, as we are describing it in this chapter, is central to the best practices of undergraduate research: "The goal is to involve students with actively contested questions, empirical observation, cutting-edge technologies, and the sense of excitement that comes from working to answer important questions" (Kuh 2008, n.p.). It is important to note within the context of the Meaningful Writing Project that Kuh's definition does prioritize the mentor, and students who described these experiences for us often took their work beyond their mentors or went to mentors with ideas. For example, one student offered this description of her meaningful writing project: "I did a summer research project under my mentor utilizing archival sources from the NYPL and the NYHS which I expanded to include an independent study the following semester." And for why that was her most meaningful project, she wrote, "I was able to research something that I was interested in, relying on the expertise of a professor that I respected." Here we see personal connection, her agency, and engagement all working together to create meaningfulness.

As our epigraph to this chapter suggests, we also heard students describe accomplishment via routes and experiences other than presentation or publication. In the "Why meaningful?" responses we coded 12 percent of all responses were accomplishment, the fifth most frequent code we assigned.

- The writing process was extremely taxing, but when I look back at that paper I am very proud of the work I turned in and the skills I acquired.

- The project was meaningful because I had to put in a ton of work in researching the subject matter, but also a lot of work went into the composition of the actual document! One of the most rewarding aspects of this project was when the final words were written down and I was able to look back at everything!

- It was meaningful because it was neat to write a short paper in a new different language. It was very rewarding to see my new ability to write fluently in a foreign language.

In the responses we coded *accomplishment,* we often saw engagement with the meaningful writing project as closely tied to writing and researching processes and to future careers:

- In combining information from a variety of fields, I was able to manipulate the information into a meaningful, important thesis that had never been considered before. The human interest of the piece made it worthwhile.
- The writing of the project I had done could benefit me in the future. I might find a career in which I will be required to do some similar experiments and write about them.

The engineering student who imagined these "similar experiments" in his future also noted the project had been his most meaningful because "it showed [his] professor that [he] had the abilities to work on the required experiments." Thus, accomplishment that comes from engagement in learning and writing builds possible future engagement with the professor—and the profession—as well. What is also clear in these responses is how student agency, engagement, and learning for transfer (the subject of our next chapter) are intertwined with students' meaningful writing projects.

Closely related to responses we coded *accomplishment* were those we coded *length* or *time* for those instances in which students made note of how long their final project was or how much time they put into it. In one instance, all three of these codes occurred together:

It was such a long project, and being dedicated to something on a daily basis for five months really took a lot of motivation and self discipline. In the end, I had a big result I was very proud of.

As some of these examples show, students' engagement with writing and research processes also figured prominently in their responses. Our code *researching to learn* occurred in 14 percent of all survey responses, the fourth most frequent response. *Writing to learn* was the fifth most frequent (tied with *accomplishment* as noted above). We also coded 12 percent of all responses, just four fewer than *writing to learn,* as *process,* or ones in which students described a specific process as contributing to their meaningful writing projects. Bundled together, these process-related responses (*researching to learn, writing to learn, process*) constitute the most frequent type of "Why meaningful?" response we saw. In their accounts, students described engaging with processes that are often new and closely tied to the genres in which they're writing, the content they're learning, and the future selves they're imagining. In an interview, an English major told the interviewer:

You know, analyzing literature, you move beyond the five-paragraph high-school writing, but only so much. You learn to develop a thesis and how to support it with three points or three points per paragraph, and it's a little robotic after a while. I've seen that throughout probably too many classes to name offhand.

Her most meaningful writing project came from research on the perspective of owners of "no-kill animal shelters." She conducted three interviews, transcribed those interviews, coded the transcripts for themes, and then situated those accounts within the literature on the rhetoric of human-animal relationships. As far as why it was most meaningful, she offered, "It was an entirely new style of writing for me. As an English major, I've mostly been doing literature analysis and that kind of thing. For this, it was new, and it was really interesting to me. It's something I didn't even know I enjoyed." For this English major, the routine of "literature analysis" had largely lost its meaning, and her research was an opportunity to engage with content, methods, and processes that offered new and interesting challenges.

We received many other responses in which students described engagement with new and challenging processes of researching and composing:

- I had to change the way I typically write. You also have to assume that the reader has no technical background and so explaining things in a concise manner becomes very important. Research papers themselves need to be clear and concise to prevent readers from becoming distracted with the conclusion you wanted to present.

- This assignment was meaningful because it not only was rigorous in the writing process, but it also required that students reflect on their disciplines (discourse communities). This assignment has affected all of my other writing projects because I am constantly mindful of audience, voice, tone, format, style, and other writing principles.

- It was the most thought-out and fleshed-out writing project I had engaged in up to that point. Despite the difficulties in composing a research paper so large, it proved rewarding to complete and doubly so to see it in print in the completed *Journal of Global Affairs.*

- This project was meaningful because it required me to further develop concise and clear writing skills that communicated a specific prescriptive policy. Further, because the assignment was to be completed as a group it required us to work together to write and edit the memo. We had to project the paper onto a screen and then discuss collectively how to improve the writing and edit the paper most effectively.

As seen in the last example, processes were often intertwined with materials, topics, classmates, and instructors, a rich, multilayered engagement that resulted in a meaningful writing project. The mutuality in these examples extends not merely to the student as learner but also to the ways classes become communities of writers and projects become preparation for professional discourse communities. Truthfully, we were excited to read these accounts. Even as (very) veteran writing teachers, we do not always have opportunities to hear how students conceive of their writing projects and the ways writing goes beyond a mere "skill" and becomes instead a means to engage with material and with others. The meaningful writing project seems to be a catalyst, a learning opportunity that taps into students' pasts, presents, and futures. Engagement seems key to leveraging that opportunity.

THE NSSE WRITING-QUESTION RESULTS VERSUS MEANINGFUL WRITING PROJECT RESPONSES

As we noted earlier in this chapter, one section of our survey offered three sets of questions that duplicated the National Survey of Student Engagement (NSSE) writing questions, allowing us to compare our results with those of the NSSE administered that same year (National Survey of Student Engagement 2012). Before we offer that comparison, some context: introduced in 1999 as a response to the need for improved assessment of student learning and a reaction to university rankings based on institutional resources rather than teaching and learning (Kuh 2009, 685), the NSSE has created a deep body of data on student engagement and its relationship to a panoply of key factors. Most recently, the Association of American Colleges and Universities' essential learning outcomes have been linked to NSSE measures of student engagement; results show that setting aside factors such as

> student background characteristics, the type of institutions attended, and other college experience, one or more of the NSSE measures of good practice in undergraduate education consistently predicted development during the first college year on multiple objective measures of student development, including effective reasoning and problem solving, well-being, inclination to inquire and lifelong learning, intercultural effectiveness, leadership, moral character, and integration of learning. (Kuh 2009, 687)

The initial NSSE included six questions that asked students about their writing, specifically how much writing they had done, whether they had composed drafts, and whether they had integrated sources. In their report on the first administration of these questions in 2008 (National Survey of Student Engagement 2008), the NSSE concluded that "writing matters" and summarized their findings:

Results affirmed that when institutions provided students with extensive, intellectually challenging writing activities, the students engaged in more deep learning activities such as analysis, synthesis, integration of ideas from various sources, and grappled more with course ideas both in and out of the classroom. In turn, students whose faculty assigned projects with these same characteristics reported greater personal, social, practical, and academic learning and development. Taken together, these findings provide further support for the movement to infuse quality writing experiences throughout the curriculum. (22)

Despite this encouraging finding for those who teach writing and administer writing programs, given the limited scope of the questions, responses offered only a partial view of what "quality writing experiences" might look like (Paine et al. 2015, 173). To address this need, in 2008 the NSSE and the Council of Writing Program Administrators (CWPA) together formed the Consortium for the Study of Writing in College and then sought input from CWPA members to develop "a consensus model for effective practices in writing" (Anderson et al. 2015, 206). The result was twenty-seven writing questions for NSSE-participating institutions to add to their survey (200).

In a 2015 *Research in the Teaching of English* article reporting "survey responses from over 70,000 first-year and senior students who were enrolled at 80 bachelor's degree-granting colleges and universities in the United States" (Anderson et al. 2015, 204) on the twenty-seven NSSE writing questions, and who completed the NSSE in 2010 and 2011 (212), Paul Anderson, Chris Anson, Bob Gonyea and Chuck Paine separate the NSSE writing questions into a conceptual model of "three effective writing practices"—"Interactive Writing Processes," "Meaning-Making Writing Tasks," and "Clear Writing Expectations" (209). They then conduct statistical analyses to show that the practices that underlie these three constructs "are associated with students' engagement in deep learning activities" and that merely how much students write is not (222). Overall, Anderson et al. conclude that "first-year students and seniors whose writing assignments involved interactive processes and provided clear expectations were more likely to perceive greater progress in learning and development" (224).

Given the important work being conducted on the relationship between engagement as defined in the NSSE and student writing—and the work of the Consortium for the Study of Writing in College—we added three sets of NSSE writing questions to our student survey so we might draw comparisons between the NSSE results and our student-survey participants. These three sets of questions focused on (1) the processes students used to write their meaningful writing projects, (2) the kind of writing students did, and (3) the role of their instructors in meaningful writing project composing (see app. B). To draw our comparison, we focused on the 2012 NSSE results for seniors (approximately 5,800 total respondents), given that the meaningful writing project survey was also administered to our seniors in 2012.[3] One factor makes the comparison between our results and NSSE results a bit tricky, however: in the NSSE writing questions, students were given a five-point scale to indicate for how many of their writing assignments they engaged in particular activities (e.g., peer review, analyzing something they read, or writing short pieces of ungraded writing): no writing assignments, few writing assignments, some writing assignments, most writing assignments, or all writing assignments. In our meaningful writing project survey, we asked students to indicate *yes* or *no* if they had the particular experiences named in regard to the writing projects they indicated as most meaningful. For example, if they said they engaged in peer review, they also indicated whether the peer review was part of the process for the meaningful writing project they named. We show in figures 3.1–3.3 only the total of NSSE results marked *All assignments* or *Most assignments*. We realize we might be comparing our students' meaningful writing projects with NSSE respondents' nonmeaningful writing responses (e.g., a student who marked *few assignments* could still have experienced their meaningful writing project with one of those assignments), but given the conclusions NSSE has drawn based on its results, we thought it worthwhile to explore the comparison.

In figure 3.1, we show the comparison for the set of NSSE writing questions on the processes students used in their composing. Note that meaningful writing project respondents were more likely to engage in each of these practices except for "Used an online tutoring service" (and all differences are statistically significant at $p < .05$). We also note the quite large differences for meaningful writing project respondents in terms of the composing processes that have become common practice from first-year writing to writing-intensive classes: engaging in invention activities via brainstorming or conversation with an instructor and getting feedback from peers or teachers. Thus, in our survey, seniors were not merely reporting on writing they found most meaningful but were telling us their composing of these projects more often demonstrated the kinds of activities we actively promote in our classes as compared to the writing reported by seniors in the 2012 NSSE results.

---

[3] Our thanks to Robert Gonyea, who shared these data with us.

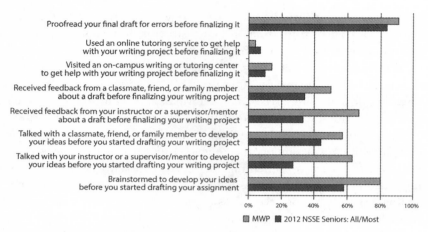

Figure 3.1. Senior responses from 2012 NSSE writing questions compared to meaningful writing project responses focusing on writing practices. (Note: All differences are statistically significant at p < .05.)

The next set of NSSE writing questions concerns the type of writing students did, whether in particular modes of discourse or with the use of particular technologies. Once again, as shown in figure 3.2, we saw statistically significant differences between the seniors describing their meaningful writing projects and the seniors who completed the NSSE. Of particular note are the much greater percentages of meaningful writing project seniors who reported they narrated or described their experience in their meaningful writing projects, as well as those who analyzed or evaluated and summarized something they read. We see these findings as related to the prevalence of *personal connection* in our coding of "Why meaningful?" (though as we noted in previous chapters, that response did not often mean students were writing about themselves or their experiences). We also see the ways meaningful writing projects were often rooted in source material, whether primary or secondary sources. We do need to note that meaningful writing projects were less likely to be created with multimedia (though they were more likely to include visual elements) as compared to NSSE findings, perhaps an indication that multimodal composing is still in a nascent stage for many student writers and their teachers at our institutions.

The third set of NSSE writing questions focuses on the role the instructor played in supporting writing. As shown in figure 3.3, once again meaningful writing project responses are all greater (and statistically significant at p < .05) than NSSE responses except for "Explained in advance what they wanted you to learn" and "Explained in advance

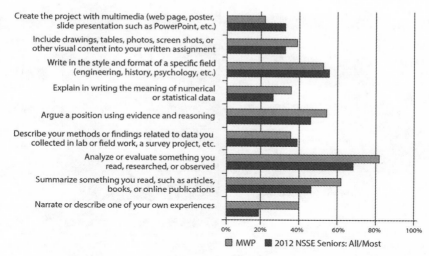

Create the project with multimedia (web page, poster, slide presentation such as PowerPoint, etc.)

Include drawings, tables, photos, screen shots, or other visual content into your written assignment

Write in the style and format of a specific field (engineering, history, psychology, etc.)

Explain in writing the meaning of numerical or statistical data

Argue a position using evidence and reasoning

Describe your methods or findings related to data you collected in lab or field work, a survey project, etc.

Analyze or evaluate something you read, researched, or observed

Summarize something you read, such as articles, books, or online publications

Narrate or describe one of your own experiences

0%   20%   40%   60%   80%   100%

▧ MWP   ▦ 2012 NSSE Seniors: All/Most

Figure 3.2. Senior responses from 2012 NSSE writing questions compared to meaningful writing project responses focusing on types of writing. (Note: All differences are statistically significant at p < .05 except for "Summarize something you read" and "Writing in the style and format of a specific field." "Describe your methods or findings related to data" is significant at p < .10.)

the criteria they would use to grade your writing project" (which is statistically significant at p < .10). While we focus on instructor perspectives in chapter 5, based on students' perspectives, instructors in classes in which the meaningful writing project occurred were more likely to use informal, nongraded writing, to have students invoke an audience for their writing, and to have students engage in peer review compared to NSSE respondents. In other words, as was true for the writing-process questions, students' instructors in their classes in which the meaningful writing project took place were more likely to exhibit the practices most familiar to those of us teaching writing as compared to NSSE respondents' instructors.

Given the overwhelming data supporting the relationship between engagement and student learning (and other positive outcomes) and the research supporting the relationship between writing and engagement, what does our comparison of NSSE writing-question results and meaningful writing project survey results offer? We can say that on twenty, or 80 percent, of the twenty-five questions listed in figures 3.1 to 3.3, Meaningful Writing Project respondents were more likely to have engaged in the composing practices and experienced the teaching practices the field of composition studies has put forth as ideal (i.e., these

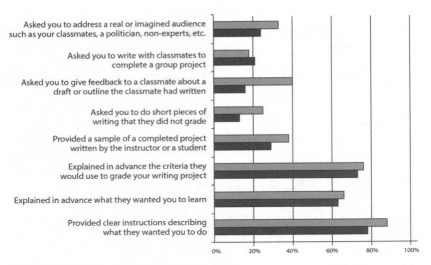

Figure 3.3. Senior responses from 2012 NSSE writing questions compared to meaningful writing project responses focusing on instructor practices. (Note: All differences are statistically significant at p < .05 except for "Explained in advance what they wanted you to learn" and "Explained in advance the criteria they would use to grade your writing project," which is statistically significant at p < .10.)

differences were statistically significant at p < .05; two other differences were statistically significant at p < .10). While we hesitate to conclude meaningful writing project writers were *more* engaged than their NSSE counterparts, we do certainly see some important things going on for the students who responded to our survey. While we saw a wide range of assignments and meaningful writing projects that occurred from students' first year to their senior year, and in required courses in and out of majors to elective courses, the conditions for engaging in best writing practices and for receiving best teaching practices seemed quite consistent. These results, we conclude, are an endorsement of those practices. Not all students had those experiences with their meaningful writing projects, but they were on the whole more likely to than the many thousands of students who filled out the NSSE and reported that all or most of their writing involved those practices. If there's a "secret sauce" for ensuring students experience meaningful writing, then, these comparisons tell us it's not so secret that these processes and practices support students' meaningful writing. Having students engage in invention activities, peer review, and instructor review; offering writing tasks that involve tapping into experience and analyzing and evaluating data or sources; and designing instruction so as to include those activities are commonplaces our writing pedagogies and research studies have long endorsed. That teaching conditions, class sizes, faculty workloads, and other structural factors severely challenge widespread offering of these practices is also well known. Our study tells us students can find deep meaning with their writing, but the comparison we've shown in this chapter tells us the conditions for achieving that meaning are not as ubiquitous as we would hope.

Before we turn to two case studies of student engagement, we want to go back to the Anderson et al. (2015) article on the NSSE writing questions and their findings that "interactive writing processes," "meaning-making writing tasks," and "clear writing expectations" had positive relationships to student learning outcomes. While we might conclude from our NSSE writing-question results that students in our study experienced those gains as well, and perhaps more so given they were more likely to engage in almost all of those activities as compared to the seniors NSSE surveyed in 2012, we also know such survey responses offer only a limited account. For example, consider this student's open-ended response following the NSSE questions on our survey:

> The instructor certainly discussed with us general things he wanted or thought we should be working on. I did not, however, check those boxes because I believe part of why the writing project was so meaningful for me was its open-endedness. He did work with us on the papers but the idea of expecting a specific structure or giving details on a very strict format or requirements would have hindered the process, I believe.

For this student, at least, the "open-endedness" or choice that enabled agency as we describe in chapter 2 precluded assigning to her instructor the responsibility for enacting the practices the survey questions asked about. She did not "check the boxes" because she felt she was in charge of her learning, and given the prevalence of choice as a key factor in why students felt their writing projects were meaningful, we wondered how many others felt as she did. Nevertheless, as Anderson et al. (2015) note from their study, "There appears to be a reasonable basis for finding a causal relationship: the more actions instructors take to explain their assignments clearly (independent variable), the more the students will report positive behaviors and perceptions (dependent variables)" (229). We explore this relationship with varied and detailed examples in chapter 5 as we offer data from the faculty who were noted for assigning students the projects that turned out to be their most meaningful. As we show, the triangulation of survey and interview data from students and their instructors offers a rich view of the interaction between engagement, student learning, and faculty intentionality.

CASE STUDIES OF MEANINGFUL WRITING PROJECTS AND ENGAGEMENT

The two case studies we chose for this chapter exemplify the social qualities of engagement we have focused on to this point: in meaningful writing projects, students engage with instructors, peers, content, and processes. In the first case, a sociology major found her meaningful writing project in an advanced disciplinary writing course in social science. In the second, an energy management major named as most meaningful a writing project in a communication class.

CASE STUDY 1—LAURIE: ENGAGING WITH INSTRUCTOR, PEERS, CONTENT, AND PROCESSES IN ADVANCED WRITING IN THE DISCIPLINES

In our first case study of *engagement* and meaningful writing projects, we focus on one particular class at Northeastern that was highly represented in our results. Advanced Writing in the Disciplines (AWD) is a required, upper-division course under the aegis of the writing program/English department. However, rather than a single course, AWD has fourteen different versions, each representing a disciplinary area (e.g., Advanced Writing in the Sciences, Advanced Writing in the Health Professions, Advanced Writing in Business, Advanced Writing in the Technical Professions; see http://www.northeastern.edu/writing/advanced-writing-in-the-disciplines/course-descriptions/ for the complete list). Instructional staff are a combination of full-time lecturers (who teach the largest number of sections), part-time lecturers, English department PhD students, and tenure-stream faculty. While the curriculum is not the same in each section, all instructors work from a shared set of student-learning goals, and many take the approach of asking students pursue a topic of interest in their fields, then present that topic via different genres and with different audiences in mind; examples might be a literature review for an academic audience, a public document for a public audience, or a white paper for a professional audience.

We focus on AWD here because it was the class most frequently cited as the source for students' meaningful writing projects: of the 271 Northeastern students who completed the survey, 70, or 26 percent, cited AWD as the course in which their meaningful writing project took place. (The next most frequent class was Biology Capstone, which was cited by six students.) Of course, one explanation is that AWD might have been the *only* course for many students in which significant writing took place, a conclusion somewhat complicated by the fact that Northeastern also has a writing-intensive-course requirement in students' majors. Nevertheless, the consistency of students' responses to "Why Meaningful?" when it came to AWD shows the class as an opportunity for engagement with content, with students' personal experiences, and with their aspirations in quite powerful ways.

All these types of engagement came into play for the student we feature here. Laurie, a sociology major, who identified on our survey as "White/Caucasian," "female," "22–25," took AWD in the fall of her junior year. In her survey response to what her meaningful writing project was and why it was meaningful, she offered the following:

> The portfolio I composed through Advanced Writing in the Disciplines with Professor N____ was quite possibly the most meaningful writing experience I've had at Northeastern. We were given the opportunity to choose a topic of interest to us and were guided through the writing process (emphasis on it as a process) to compose four polished documents each of a different genre. The professor really made the experience monumental. We had due dates for drafts, peer reviews, and final papers. We would have a class discussing the particular genre and our questions and ideas. The next class would be a workshop where we worked in groups (about 3 per group) to discuss what we had done so far and offer advice. In between we would write a review of a paper from one of the students in our group—focusing on the requirements and qualities of each genre given to us by the professor. In class we would get into our groups and discuss the peer reviews and how to improve with a focus on constructive criticism (the professor also reviewed each paper and met individually with each student). The following class the final was due and the process began anew. At the end of the four pieces, we reviewed all of them and compiled a portfolio with a reflection (also peer reviewed).
>
> Writing is really a personal experience so the fact that the professor acted as a guide rather than a dictator really facilitated my improvement throughout the class. The whole process was very student oriented; there was no textbook, every class was either an open discussion or group discussions of the writing process, experience, or pieces we had just written or reviewed. I understand that you have to be the type of person to be able to work independently (i.e. without a professor over your shoulder every step of the way moving you along) and you must put emphasis on meeting deadlines but this really worked the best for me. I was so thrilled with this course I have suggested it to many other students—meaning I suggested this professor in particular since the AWD courses vary widely across professors. Honestly, I improved and grew more in my writing through this course than in all of the other courses I have taken combined. Also, I ENJOYED it—that is saying a lot for me from an English course (prior to this I was not fond of writing at all and dreaded every paper assignment).

We coded this response *process, engagement, affect, accomplishment.*

As was true for the great majority of other survey respondents, Laurie reported she had not engaged in this type of task previously but did expect to do this kind of writing in the future. In terms of the latter, she noted:

> The topic of my choice and introduction to it and to writing about it provided me with the foundation I needed to write more in-depth on the subject in subsequent years. It is the field that I hope to go into and I now have the skills and experience to feel like I am ready to further my learning in that direction. The other way it had helped me is in the ability to review work done by a peer. The difference between editing and reviewing is extremely significant and the ability to actually write a review is priceless.

In Laurie's interview with Sara, who was at the time a sophomore English major, Laurie expands upon the content of her writing in AWD and on her engagement with her instructor, her classmates, and with the content. In terms of that topic, here's how Laurie describes to Sara what she wrote about:

> I was looking at the breast cancer movement. The first [part of the portfolio] was a description of the knowledge front, what am I actually trying to research or write about. The second one was a reference article. I actually did a *Discover Magazine* article for that one, even though it wasn't officially a reference article. I did it about environmental estrogens and their impact on causing breast cancer. The third one was a more common, general article, at eighth-grade level, like a newspaper article. That was about pink washing and the breast-cancer movement and how a lot of the chemicals aren't getting acknowledged as causing breast cancer. The final one was a critique of National Breast Cancer Awareness Month and its involvement in that process.

In terms of engagement with her instructor, Laurie makes clear to Sara the role her instructor played in the course: "I think that at least 50 or 60 percent of why it was meaningful had to do with how it was organized, and that was pretty much all the professor." This organization extended to the processes her instructor established for the completion of the portfolio and to the rounds of class discussion and peer review Laurie relied on to refine her work. As Laurie described, "Just the whole environment of the class, the process, and the dates, and everything was helpful. . . . I think that was one of the greatest courses that I've ever had, and I never ever liked English or writing before that. It was awesome."

As we saw in many students' responses, Laurie found her instructor struck the right balance between required elements and student choice. This balance extended to how she structured peer review:

I think [the success of the class] also had to do with the students. I mean, some of the students were more into it than others, I think. The environment of the class was like, you are responsible for your own writing process. I mean she helped you and guided you, but she didn't say like specifically, "This. You have to do this." I mean it was like, "Well this is when it's due. If you need to have a peer review done by this point or whatever." And then, it was your responsibility to get it in by that point, and she was always there, and she had a class where when we did the peer-review discussions, we'd move around and have time to talk with her. She would come to each group and answer questions or whatever.

An aspect Laurie thought was particularly important for making this project meaningful was the extended time—essentially an entire semester—spent in exploration of her topic of choice but considered from various points of view and presented in various genres. In her interview, Laurie contrasted this experience in AWD with other courses that included required writing projects: "I think that since other courses go so quickly that you don't have time to really focus on the writing as a process, which, of course, is the focus of the advanced writing course." Another contrast with other courses was the way she and her AWD classmates engaged in the processes of drafting, revision, and peer review throughout the semester rather than simply turning in a final paper:

I've had other courses where you work on one project for the whole semester, which is helpful, and then you can delve really deep into it. But on the other hand, unless you have, like, assigned—you have to turn in a draft, you get feedback from your peers, you get feedback from the professor, you have to do this—throughout the semester, it doesn't really help you because then people do it all at the end. It's not really a process, it's just a one-time thing.

Ultimately, Laurie saw her writing in AWD as useful for courses in her major she took in subsequent semesters, as well as for her future writing. In terms of the former, she noted she continued to focus on the topic of breast-cancer awareness in classes in which she was able to choose her own topic, thus feeling she had "all that base knowledge and the base writing skills." Laurie felt the project would continue to be useful after graduation, noting, "I want to go into environmental health, and it provided a foundation for that." Laurie also focused on the reflection component of her AWD portfolio as particularly important for future writing, explaining that her instructor "framed the reflection" as preparation for personal statements in graduate-school or scholarship applications" and that students might "reform or adapt the question that they pose to be more about your writing process, and then answer it. So, it's almost like a practice. It's a reflection and a practice for future applications and stuff you do." The experience is also an example of what we describe in the next chapter as *learning for transfer*—which begins when the articulation of experiences, accomplishments, goals, and challenges contributes to formulations of a future writerly self.

Overall, Laurie's engagement in AWD—exploring a topic of her choice through a series of interrelated writing tasks, engaging in multiple rounds of revision and peer review carefully orchestrated by her instructor— was echoed in many other Northeastern students' survey and interview responses when the site for their meaningful writing project was AWD. While a required, upper-division disciplinary writing course might not be the right fit for every institution, the mutual engagement with content, processes, peers, and instructors these students described offers a power- ful model of student learning, one that does not strike us as extraordinary or difficult to replicate. As we described in terms of the NSSE writing ques- tions, the teaching and learning practices writing studies has long advo- cated do, indeed, lead to meaningful writing projects. The challenge, of course, is creating the conditions for those practices to thrive.

CASE STUDY 2—YVES: "PICTURING MYSELF IN THE PROFESSIONAL WORLD" THROUGH BUSINESS COMMUNICATION AND ENGAGEMENT WITH THE COMMUNITY

Our second case study also describes a student's experiences in an ad- vanced required writing course, in this case a class for business majors. The student clearly valued the outcomes of the project and the social engagement he experienced. However, he also recognized how being a non-native English speaker and international student may have impact- ed his experience with writing and with his instructor.

Yves, an energy management major, identified on our survey as "Male," "Black/African American," and "30 and over," and in his inter- view he noted he is an international student from Western Africa. Yves described his meaningful writing project, which he wrote when he was a sophomore: "I wrote the report entitled 'Improving Cleveland Area Rap- id Transit (CART) Ridership' for my business communication class. . . . I studied why CART ridership decreased 10% in 2010 and came up with a short list of causes and advocated a few solutions to permanently fix this downturn." As to why the project was meaningful, he offered, "Because I take CART to campus every day and I had a chance to experience di- rectly a few discrepancies." We coded this response *app+* and *personal connection*, but when Yves was interviewed by two first-year students, their questions led to many more details about how he engaged with others, including representatives of the transportation company and his professor, as he researched and wrote his project. Yves's interaction also included administering a survey of transit use to his fellow students and gathering "a few thousand" responses.

Although Yves reported on our survey that he had never written anything like his meaningful writing project before, he imagined his meaningful writing project would engage with the kinds of writing he hoped to do in the future. He wrote: "This writing project could help me when it is time to write my master's papers. It also gave me more confidence in completing one kid's book I have been slacking on for over a year now." In a further open-ended survey question, he added: "I am more confident about my writing skills than ever before. This (gruesome) project helped me a lot."

In his interview he expands on the processes of research and writing, telling his interviewers, "We had to investigate a company to see what they do that they could do better." When one of his interviewers asks him to talk them through the process of writing the project, he offers this account:

> It was a lot of back and forth with the teacher, me and the teacher, and then, me and the company. First, I had to decide what I wanted to write about then I had to get approval from the teacher first, and then, I start gathering resources. I went to the company and I asked to talk to the PR, but she wasn't there, and then she never returned my emails. And then, I emailed somebody else who was a . . . I don't remember his title, but they emailed me the data and everything, the sales lady, all the data I needed to write this paper. We exchanged three to four emails like that.

Pushed to explain more about why the project was the one he chose, he describes the ways in which the report felt to him like something he might be responsible for developing in a future role:

> It was meaningful because I was picturing myself, like, in the professional world. Those are the kind of project, report that your boss could ask you to rewrite. I took this very seriously. It was meaningful because it was something new. But at the same time it was very, very demanding and then difficult at times. You need to gather your resources and then, you need to have the adequate level of writing English, you know, like business writing. And, then, it was a lot.

Leading up to this project were shorter projects: "Mostly we learned to write reports, like one, two pages. We learned how to write business letters, negative letters, positive letters." Yves also had quite a bit of interaction with his business communication professor through "office hours, in class, one-on-one discussion." Overall, Yves remembers "writing all the time," and he explains to his interviewers that "writing in English was already a big, big challenge" because English is not his first language.

Toward the end of the interview, when asked if there was anything else about the meaningful writing project or the process of writing it that he would like to offer, Yves describes that as an international student writing has been difficult for him. He explains: "I know the teachers want to grade. They don't, I'm sorry to say, they don't care where you're coming from." As the interviewers empathize with "yeah," he adds: "I heard many students like me, from my perspective, my background, complaining a little bit saying, 'Failed to grade outside. Come on, separate. Not at the same level like the American students.'" He tells the interviewers he believes he was graded at the same level as his student peers who are not international students, yet he adds, "I wish we could have it otherwise, but . . ." His "final report" was worth "25 percent" of his grade, and his grade was "a 80, a B," which he feels showed that his instructor liked what he wrote.

Yves's story reminds us of how conscious students are of the tension between feeling engaged with new writing experiences and their instructors' possible bias toward students' language use, their uncritical enforcement of Standard Written English, or a lack of their acknowledgment of the many Englishes students bring to bear on their writing in US classrooms (Canagarajah 2013; Inoue 2015; Poe 2013; Smitherman and Villanueva 2003). In Yves's case, that possible bias did not keep him from appreciating the context in which he learned important skills for his future. Overall, the meaningful writing project offered Yves plenty of opportunities for engagement, including with the processes of research and writing, the interactions with his peers and his teacher, and the pursuit of solutions to a community-based problem.

CONCLUSION

The social view of engagement we have offered in this chapter obviously overlaps with the elements of agency that are the focus of our previous chapter. Students' engagement with instructors, peer, materials, and processes is intertwined with their development of agency and control of their learning. Also connected are the ways in which this learning might transfer onto new contexts, which we saw repeatedly as students described an engagement with their future writerly selves. In chapter 4, we take up the topic of meaningful writing and learning for transfer.

4

LEARNING FOR TRANSFER AND THE MEANINGFUL WRITING PROJECT

This project was very meaningful for me because it combined what I have learned over the last 3 years and challenged the beliefs I previously had.
—Classical languages major

What made the project so meaningful was that it allowed me to put to use my knowledge and interest in my major. My chosen career field requires a vast amount of analytical writing, which has become of great interest to me. By offering me the opportunity to write such a paper has allowed me to explore whether or not I am choosing the right career path.
—Government and politics and psychology major

In the previous two chapters, we examined students' meaningful writing projects via the frameworks of agency and engagement. In this chapter, we offer an additional framework—learning for transfer—that emerged from our data through inductive analysis and that also responds to current conversations in writing studies and educational research more generally. In terms of those larger conversations, during the period of time in which we collected and analyzed our data, the Elon University Research Seminar, "Critical Transitions: Writing and the Question of Transfer," took place,[4] and several key texts were published on the topic, including a 2012 issue of *Composition Forum* reporting on the Elon researchers' findings, Nowacek's (2011) *Agents of Integration: Understanding Transfer as a Rhetorical Act*, and Yancey, Robertson, and Taczak's (2014) *Writing Across Contexts: Transfer, Composition, and Sites of Writing*. A central premise of our study is that we have too often focused on how our writing instruction might produce "outcomes" while paying little attention to the considerable skills, knowledge, and dispositions—or "incomes" (Guerra 2008) and "discursive resources" (Guerra 2015)—students bring to our classrooms, writing centers, and other learning spaces. The research on transfer, similarly, is concerned with what students bring to a new learning situation or, more specifically, how prior learning does and does not impact new learning. In this chapter

---

[4] See http://www.elon.edu/e-web/academics/teaching/ers/writing_transfer/.

DOI: 10.7330/9781607325802.c004

we hope to add to this conversation from what we have learned from students' descriptions of their meaningful writing projects.

In their many studies, David Perkins and Gavriel Salomon, who are often cited by writing studies researchers, restate the challenge of pinpointing learning transfer due to differences between local and global knowledges, the "fuzziness of disciplines," and the unpredictability of future contexts, but one message is clear: "When conditions *are* met, useful transfer from one context to another often occurs" (Perkins and Salomon 1989, 22). As we have analyzed what students told us about their most meaningful writing projects, we have tried to understand and reconstruct the "conditions" necessary for "useful transfer" into—or outward from—their meaningful writing projects: What did the assignment ask for? Had students done something like that before? How might the task connect to students' interests and passions? Do they see how they might do that type of writing in the future?

While we assumed students would name writing as meaningful if they were working from genres with which they were familiar, one finding of our survey results surprised us: we found that nearly 80 percent of students identified their meaningful writing project as a *new* writing experience. What was not new, however, were the ways students used what we coded *personal connection* to build relationships between previous experiences and their meaningful writing projects. What these students viewed as first-time opportunities would lead to similar opportunities in the future: as we point out in our chapter on agency, 69 percent of students surveyed believed their most meaningful writing projects were the kind of writing they might do postgraduation, predicting a continued exploration of identity and personal connection they discovered in their meaningful writing projects. Thus, what we often heard students describing were the ways the meaningful writing project represented a link to the past via a resonant personal connection and a bridge to the future via the applicability or relevance of the projects.

In what follows, we offer results from our surveys and interviews to describe the ways we saw transfer operating (or not operating) for students in our study: the role of new writing challenges, the ways meaningful writing projects connect to students' prior interests and passions, and students' beliefs that their meaningful writing projects would play a role in future writing. We then consider what our study reveals about the learning and teaching that can lead to transfer, focusing on how learning and teaching contexts that foster "expansive framing" (Engle et al. 2012) may best support both meaningful writing and opportunities for writers to learn for transfer.

THE POWER OF *NEW*

As we just described, one prominent finding in our research reveals the power of new experiences and new opportunities for students. In our student survey, we asked the following question: "For the project you've described as meaningful, had you previously written anything similar?" Across 707 survey respondents and three different institutions, 79 percent, or nearly eight out of ten students, reported they had not written anything similar.

Consistently and emphatically, the newness of the meaningful writing project comes across as key to its meaningfulness. In the survey, students told us about many firsts:

- Because I have never written anything like that before, I found it freeing and also challenging.
- I had been working with non-profits for many, many years. I had never had the chance to learn what it would take to actually start one.
- This project was meaningful to me mostly because of its purpose, which was to provide a condensed source of vital information to survivors of sexual and domestic abuse. It was also meaningful to me because it was one of the first professional projects I worked on independently involving research and in-depth writing.
- It was the first large technical report I had to write that pertained to my major. I felt highly accomplished once I handed the report in.

It was a new challenge, a new opportunity to learn something, whether content or genre or process; or a new opportunity to connect to a passion or previous content knowledge; or the first time to engage with faculty and peers. Of course, that does not mean students did not bring any prior knowledge to their chosen meaningful writing projects, particularly when knowledge is broadened to include Beaufort's (2007) five knowledge domains (knowledge of writing process, discourse community, rhetorical context, content, and genre) as well as affective domains (Driscoll and Wells 2012; Perkins and Salomon 2012). Certainly, some repurposing of prior learning (Wardle 2007; Yancey et al. 2014) was happening here, but simply replicating previous writing was never cited as a meaningful writing project. That sort of transfer did not occur. (In fact, replicating the same writing over and over again is exactly what a number of the students who went out of their way to tell us they had no meaningful writing projects in their time as undergraduates described as their experience.) While Susan Ambrose et al. (2010) found that "the more dissimilar the learning and transfer contexts, the less likely transfer will occur" (108), our findings instead urge us to look carefully at the intersection of students' meaningful writing projects, their identification of it as a *new* experience, and the perception of transfer of knowledge in or application out.

We particularly saw the power of *new* in the ways students consistently told us their meaningful writing projects offered opportunities to learn new content. These responses, which we coded as *content learning*, occurred in 21 percent of all survey responses. In some instances, in response to the question about why they believed a project was meaningful, students simply told us what they had been learning:

- Learning about hysteria and how women felt with the presumed guilt.
- No innocent person should be put in prison and have their life pass them by. They lose so much time that could have been with their family that they will never get back, while the guilty person is walking free.
- The paper made me look at another side of film, an expressionistic side where the visuals didn't just signify moving the plot forward.

In addition to learning new content, in survey responses and interviews, students told us about opportunities to research and write new genres. For example, one of our interview participants, Sara, an English major, told us about an ethnography project she chose as her most meaningful and how this new writing offered a welcome break from what had become routine in her literary analysis papers:

> [My meaningful writing project] was an entirely new style of writing for me. As an English major, I've mostly been doing literature analysis and that kind of thing. . . . I can bang out an English paper like nobody's business. . . . It's not really challenging anymore. . . . For this, it was new and it was really interesting to me. It's something I didn't even know I enjoyed. . . . I think it was the difference between looking at a piece of writing and analyzing it, and looking at the real life interaction with another person that I really enjoyed.

And sometimes the opportunity to learn new content or theory or method and put that learning to use marked a recognizable turning point in a student's undergraduate experience. For example, a student who described her meaningful writing project as "basically extracting a rhetorical theory from a feminist philosopher whom I read" said the project was her most meaningful because "it was the first real opportunity [she] had in [her] education to write a paper strongly based on feminist ideas for the sake of them. Any other times [she] wrote things that may have involved feminist theory, it was in a subservient way because the course did not allow for such variations." In other words, as she told us in her yes/no answer, she had never written anything like this project before. Asked if she hoped to write in a similar way in the future, she said "yes" and offered this additional open-ended response:

Since this project, I have continued to try to include feminist theory or ideas into my writing and have become better at involving it significantly, regardless of feminist influence on the course. I imagine, as I get my masters, I will continue to do this, and perhaps have opportunities again to write entirely on feminist theory for the sake of it.

Her responses to all of our survey questions show how complicated *new* can be. While using feminist theory in her writing may not have been entirely new for this student when she wrote her meaningful writing project, using feminist theory in a newly agentive way contributed to building her meaningful writing project. And "regardless of feminist influence on the course," her sense of agency following the meaningful writing project is what allows her to transfer her content knowledge and rhetorical skill forward.

TRANSFER IN—THE POWER OF *PERSONAL CONNECTION*

As the previous student's story reveals, while the tasks for meaningful writing projects might have been new for most students, we did see a strong connection to prior knowledge and experiences. The most prevalent code we found among students' survey answers for why they chose a project as meaningful was one we labeled *personal connection*, which occurred in 36 percent of all responses. While this term might at a glance seem to indicate that the meaningful writing project allowed students to write about themselves in some way, autobiography/personal narrative was a fairly rare genre in students' accounts. Instead, *personal connection* represented an opportunity to connect personally to the writing project, whether that connection came through a passion for the subject, a previous experience, or a sense of developing disciplinary identity.

In terms of passion or connection to the topic, consider the following survey responses:

- I had always liked that memorial in the park, and being able to sit and write a paper on how it was interpreted by others and the community around it gave new meaning to the location for me.
- Writing about what was the meaning behind the company and the company's actions and output was inspiring to me. The assignment reconfirmed the reason why I want to be in business. I want to make a difference with what business practices I follow and how I provide a certain good or service to consumers.
- Anti-human trafficking is an important issue to me, so being able to write a report that allowed me to explore the issue more was very meaningful.

- The attack of September 11 really affected me and to reflect about the new WTC seems to be the most meaningful in all of the papers I wrote for classes.

In each of these responses, the connection to prior knowledge or prior interests/passions is clear, and the meaningful writing project offered an opportunity to make those connections and allowed a student to capitalize on those interests/passions. In an interview, one student attested to the power of the passion one has for a topic to be a driving force, particularly in a school context where external requirements such as page length and grades play a powerful role:

> I like being able to have a topic that is of interest to me because I know that I don't have to worry about the page length. I don't have to worry about, "Do I have enough paragraphs?" I just focus on what the context of the paper is. I've always been interested in disabilities and children with disabilities. A lot of times I would write the paper on that. I would just go and write for pages and pages. I didn't even care what the grade was because it was so passionate to me that I never had a problem with it.

As we mentioned in chapter 1, a toxicology student, Ben, surprised his interviewer by explaining that the most meaningful writing project of his undergraduate years was worth just 5 percent of his overall grade. In his exchange with his peer interviewer, Ben also offered insight into the powerful relationship among his interests and his future goals and thus his motivation to engage with the meaningful writing project:

> *Ben:* Most of the papers that I write I do well on. This paper was different because, I guess don't want to admit this, but I tried a lot harder on this paper than I have on other papers where I did probably equally as well. I don't know why that is.

> *Interviewer:* You don't?

> *Ben:* Yeah. I had another difficult paper that was like ten pages I didn't do so hot on. I called it my ten-page book report because he only let us use the book that we read as the source for that. That one was pretty difficult to do.

> *Interviewer:* What made this one different than that one, just like the way you . . . ?

> *Ben:* Just interest. The other one was on ancient China. It was my history class. This one was more relevant towards what I want to do, and I kind of took this as a practice to the kind of writing that I'll actually have to start to get used to doing.

> *Interviewer:* What kind of writing is that?

> *Ben:* Publishing lab results for journals and making sure that it's written in a way that the journal would want to accept your article into it.

The interests Ben brought to the project combined with what he hoped he would be doing in the future and led him to exert more effort and time on the meaningful writing project and thus to feel more engaged in this project than in other projects that went "equally as well" for him as a student.

For many students, a connection to the meaningful writing project was personal in that it invoked family, friends, or issues around identity:

- The project was meaningful for me because there aren't many cancer treatments that are both safe and effective, and I had recently seen my grandmother go through cancer treatment.
- I was an engineer for the army and have had several family members in the military. It was nice to get interviews and first-hand accounts.
- I found it meaningful because I chose to write about *commotio cordis*, an injury that a high school classmate passed away from.
- The project helped me find myself. Though I did a lighthearted topic and made it a little more of a joke than anything, I felt it to be rewarding.
- I have always been a bit of an environmentalist, as I was raised by permaculturists, so this project hit home. It also helped me think outside of the box. It also was my first research paper in 3 years.

Personal connection, then, offers a powerful means of conceptualizing transfer and is a potential bridge between students' interests in and experience with a topic and the kind of writing they identify as meaningful. Still, as indicated in many responses, students described this opportunity to make a personal connection as relatively rare in their school experiences:

- It was the first time a professor went out of their way to make sure each student was writing about something they were passionate about.
- I was able to pick my own topic to focus on. This allowed me to be engaged with my own work and actually care about the things I was writing about.
- It was something I had spent a lot of time working on and I actually cared about the specific data and topic.
- They were academic papers but it was in a subject that I felt passionate about.

These not-so-veiled critiques of assignments that do not lead to meaningful writing are quite telling, offering considerable evidence that meaningful writing projects are unfortunately scarce for students. In other words, the opportunity to connect to student "incomes" through writing are often lost. In an interview, Duran described the contrast he saw between typical assigned writing and assignments that lead to meaningful writing projects:

> Usually the prompts are pretty strict and pretty cut and dry. There's really no wiggle room. A lot of people don't like that . . . it's like playing in someone else's sandbox. You go there and you've got to know these rules and you can't do this, you can't do that, you've got to do this, this is the right way. If you get your own sandbox to do this stuff in, then you're more apt to have fun with it.

Duran experienced what Theresa Lillis (2002) describes as the dominant experience of students in higher education (HE). As she writes, "It is difficult to get close to individual desires for meaning making within the context of the culture of HE: student-writers' efforts are inevitably channeled into working out what is acceptable with HE, rather than exploring what they might want to mean" (45).

Of course, some students took a more optimistic view of these prior experiences, a kind of take-your-medicine approach they saw as good for them "in the long run," as Shamim told us in an interview:

> Some papers I've had to write I was yawning every five seconds because they were so boring. But in the long run I don't regret writing them. Any assignments that I've had to really do in college, as stupid and pointless as it was, I'm glad I did it. Really, I'm actually glad that I was almost forced against my will to write hundreds of papers because they really helped me in the end.

TRANSFER IN—PRIOR KNOWLEDGE AND THE MEANINGFUL WRITING PROJECT

While *personal connection* offers one lens to view the relationship between transfer and prior learning, students were also quite detailed in their descriptions of their meaningful writing project as an opportunity to use content or writing knowledge they had learned previously. In these responses we coded as *transfer*, students described strategies, skills, or knowledge they transferred to their meaningful writing projects. In addition, when students described the meaningful writing project as an opportunity to view a previous outside-of-school experience or topic with an academic or analytical lens, we coded these responses *re-see*, another type of transfer or use of prior knowledge. Though these codes (*transfer* and *re-see*) added up to only 8 percent of all responses, for those students, the meaningful writing project was synthetic and analytic in a certain sense or offered an opportunity to synthesize or analyze prior learning or prior experience:

- What made the project so meaningful was that it allowed me to put to use my knowledge and interest in my major.
- I have been working with nonprofits for many, many years. I had never had to the chance to learn what it would take to actually start one.
- This class and assignment has brought loose ends together in summing up the business world.
- It was the first time I'd ever done anything that long or in-depth so I felt like I was really putting what I'd learned to use.
- Challenged my existing thoughts and ideas. Made me think and write creatively.

Our interview with Jessica reflected this opportunity to connect to previous learning or previous writing experiences:

> [It] was really exciting for me to actually get to do research on the things that I had been doing in my co-op. One, I already felt comfortable with them. At the time I was really sure that was what I wanted to do with my career. I felt like I was really learning a lot for something that I wanted to be learning about and I really wanted to do after school.

Similarly, Kristine described how her previous coursework prepared her for the writing she did for her meaningful writing project:

> I think the honors classes I took did [prepare me] because they all expected the same level of writing. Not necessarily as in depth but the same kind of analysis. *Level* is probably the best word, it's a high level. You're expected to understand what you're talking about and not just fake your way through it.

We should also point out that while 79 percent of survey respondents reported not having written anything similar to their meaningful writing projects, that leaves 21 percent of respondents who did. For this group, as they described those previous writing projects, we could see a particular kind of transfer taking place, one that was usually focused on particular genres of writing or an early opportunity to explore the topic they would later take up in their meaningful writing projects:

- I had to do a very similar project, except this time wasn't a whole profile, it was just an interview.
- In high school, same topic, less research.
- I had written several other papers involving similar concepts in politics.
- As a senior in high school, I wrote a similar personal statement for my application for college, and as a sophomore in college I wrote a similar paper as part of a job application.
- The fact that it was personal and that I had to use ALL my creative writing skills in order to succeed in the project.

One might imagine that students describing these opportunities to build on previous knowledge and experiences might come up with different reasons for choosing a writing project as most meaningful. However, for this group, the code *personal connection* was still the most frequent, found in 37 percent of these responses, slightly higher than the 36 percent frequency rate we found for all survey responses. In other words, students' most dominant reason for choosing a writing project as most meaningful was consistent across these two groups: the 79 percent of students who did not feel they had written anything similar and the 21 percent of student who did. Thus, personal connection as the mechanism for transfer in our study was quite striking.

TRANSFER FORWARD—THE HOPE FOR FUTURE RELEVANCY

Students' future contexts—or more specifically what students saw as the relationship between their meaningful writing projects and future writing—were easier for them to imagine as possible explicit sites for transfer. When we asked in our survey, "Are there any ways in which this writing project might contribute to the kinds of writing you hope to do in the future?," 69 percent of students believed that their meaningful writing projects would transfer to future writing. Thus, rather than a "carry and unload" (Wardle 2007) view of transfer, from students' perspectives, transfer is potentially important when considering future writing, particularly writing connected to who they expect to be and become and to the kinds of writing they expect to encounter.

In her interview, Jessica further described applying the genre knowledge she developed in her meaningful writing project to the writing she would do in her capstone course:

> I'm glad that I had that experience because I wouldn't have been able to have done it as successfully for my capstone if I hadn't had very specific practice doing a literature review. . . . That's good because I got really good practice doing [a] literature review and really wrapping my head around what that means because half of the kids in my seminar have never done one before. It's like a weird concept [for them].

Thus, for Jessica, this type of writing was practice for more complex writing situations she might encounter in her future.

For the 69 percent of students who answered "yes" to the survey question of whether their meaningful writing project would be reflected in future writing, we asked them to describe and be specific about what those future projects might look like. Many students had a clear view of what this future writing might look like:

- I want to take my analytic abilities elsewhere and apply them in the world! It really has given me the tool to take my skills other places.

- The lab report will help me write technical reports in the future, and if I decide to go to graduate school, it will help with my dissertations/ theses. It taught me how to write technically, and how to write in a long form.

- As a physician assistant I will have to write referral letters to other physicians, physician assistants, and health professionals to detail them about the status of our mutual patients. This is a particular writing skill that is vital for me to master and I felt that this writing project allowed me to mentally prepare myself for this important professional writing.

- Not necessarily the kinds of writing, but it helped motivate me in what I want to do to be a successful educator.

- It was research based and provided insight on how I can be the best nurse I can be in providing culturally competent care to my patients.

The last two responses, in particular, are examples of students' perspectives on transfer that are not necessarily about strategies or skills for particular genres of writing but instead are tied more fully to issues of identity, or who students want to be and become. What seniors told us about how they can imagine writing functioning in their futures may also ask us to enlarge our notions of how writing might work for students once they graduate. Students' desired outcomes for their work with writing may or may not align with our goals. Consider the last response of the previous section in which a student described why a sophomore-year English project was his most meaningful: "The fact that it was personal and that I had to use ALL my creative writing skills in order to succeed in the project." Asked if this project might contribute to writing he'd like to do in his future, the accounting major wrote, "I'd like to do more creative writing in my personal life. It helps me expand my vocabulary." When we are focused only on the future disciplinary and professional uses of students' undergraduate writing experiences, we may miss important sites and opportunities students recognize for transfer.

Hope for the future relevancy of writing was reinforced by students' survey responses to the question about why they chose a particular writing project as most meaningful. Specifically, our second-most-frequent code for these survey responses, occurring in 34 percent of all responses, was one we labeled *app+*, which includes the concepts of *application, relevancy, future, pragmatic, authentic*, and *professionalism* as in the following responses:

- I liked the project because it allowed me to read scientific papers, which is what I will need to do for my career. It also helped me to improve my scientific writing skills, which I will need.

- The papers allowed us to experience what writing in our field would be like in the future. Also, they are about a subject that I love so researching and writing on a topic was entertaining.
- It was a difficult paper with high grading standards. But it was very relevant to my degree field covering a topic I am passionate about.
- It was relevant to my major and to the material being covered in the course. It helped me to develop a deeper understanding of the material being covered in the course. Most importantly, it is something that I (or other accounting majors) very likely will have to do at some point when we enter the workforce.
- As a student who is passionate about the environment, I was able to research in depth the actions that had been taken to respond to the issue, and to discuss the plans of officials to deal with the issue in the future. Not only was my paper relevant to my interests, but I was able to gain a better understanding of the workings of real-world agencies set up to deal with similar issues.

In these responses, students connected their meaningful writing projects to existing passions, future writing, and future identities. What students were telling us through the survey and interviews is in accord with what Jessica Lindenman offers in a study of transfer: "Students are not opposed to or unable to connect their writings in meaningful cross-contextual patterns; they only need the space to look more closely and the freedom to see their texts through their own eyes. This shift in focus has the potential to unlock a plethora of transferrable knowledge that would otherwise lie dormant" (Lindenman 2015, 14). The search for that "space" and the ways to create it have been the focus of a great deal of writing studies literature on transfer, and we next turn to that material to explore how students' meaningful writing projects might contribute to our understanding of transfer.

WRITING STUDIES AND TRANSFER

Writing studies scholars who have explored transfer often register particular unease with terminology. Elizabeth Wardle (2012) tells us that "the continued use of the word 'transfer' limits our ability to think more fully about this phenomenon and what it means" (n.p.) and instead uses "creative repurposing for expansive learning" or, in short, "repurposing" (n.p.). Rebecca Nowacek (2011) favors "transformation" over "transfer," and King Beach (1999), coming from a sociocognitive perspective, prefers "transition." Whatever the specific terminology, the literature from a writing studies perspective seems primarily concerned with *what* and *how* students learn to write in largely school-based contexts with a reoccurring emphasis on what students take away from first-year writing classes. We did not specifically use any of the terms above in our survey or interview questions, although, as we've discussed in this chapter, we did ask seniors two complementary questions: "For the project you've described as meaningful, had you previously written anything similar?" "For the project you've described as meaningful, are there ways in which this writing project might contribute to the kinds of writing you hope to do in the future?" And as we described previously, eight in ten answered "no" to the first, and nearly seven in ten answered "yes" to the second.

Although there's been little agreement on the nearly eight terms for writing and transfer, writing studies researchers have understandably remained interested in the downstream effects of writing instruction on students' future writing experiences. As Jessie Moore (2012) overviews, studies have focused on "students' transitions from first-year composition (FYC) to subsequent or concurrent contexts" (4). Few studies have actually asked students explicitly what they think they learned about writing that they can apply in other classes. But, naturally, one limitation of doing more studies with student perceptions is acknowledged by David Smit (2004): often, novice writers "do not see the relevance of what they have learned" (6)—this kind of awareness takes time, the opportunities for application are not always available at the optimal time, and few of us actually teach to activate prior knowledge in deliberate ways.

One aspect of transfer forward that has drawn attention from researchers and curriculum designers is students' development of "writing talk," or students' use of the vocabulary of writing studies. Several transfer researchers have identified the development of such language as key to successful transfer and have considered the elements of assignment design and classroom context that have and have not led to student success. For example, drawing on prior research about the power of reflection and metacognition, Kathleen Blake Yancey, Liane Robertson, and Kara Taczak designed their teaching-for-transfer curriculum with the goal of students developing a theory of writing and the language to articulate that theory. While Yancey, Robertson, and Taczak (2014) accept that "students actively use their prior knowledge," especially their prior writing knowledge, they also maintain that "while some prior knowledge provides help for new writing situations, other prior knowledge does not and can even present hurdles" (13), a finding consistent with Ambrose et al. (2010). The "teaching-for-transfer" (TFT) curriculum prioritizes students developing particular ways of describing their writing practices: "By focusing on key terms and reflection, students engage in both theory and practice about writing, which allows for the development of a theory of writing—or a framework of writing knowledge they can apply to new writing contexts—both within the course and beyond it" (73). However, we are struck that in *Writing Across Contexts*, when Yancey, Robertson, and Taczak (2014) offer a case study of Marta, a student in a composition course with a teaching-for-transfer curriculum "who identified as a writer" (89), they critique the ways she reflects on her own process because they believe she "did not employ or think in terms of the key terms linking assignments in the TFT course" (89). They write, "Marta's focus remained on the process of writing rather than on a theoretically informed practice of writing," and they imagine that since "Marta had enjoyed writing success in the past, and because that success had been validated by others, she either did not recognize or chose to ignore the writing concepts in the TFT course" (89–90). While Yancey, Robertson, and Taczak situate Marta's failure in relation to her unwillingness to engage in "*mindful transfer* of any of the larger concepts of writing from the FYC course to post-composition writing" (91), and, drawing on Perkins and Salomon (1992), imagine her stuck in "*low-road transfer* to new writing situations" (91), we are left thinking that the TFT curriculum might not align with Marta's sense of writerly agency. Is it that she fails to learn the TFT curriculum and thus fails to transfer, or is it that she is poised to become what Nowacek (2011) would call an "agent of integration," and within the TFT curriculum she just hadn't yet read her audience well enough to "sell" and/or couldn't "recalibrate that audience's expectations" (39) to value what she was offering? As we are interested in what students do to reach their own goals, we think of Nowacek (2011), who writes that "some agents reconfigure the discursive space within which they operate in order to achieve their own goals, not simply the goals articulated for them by others" (40). It seems to us that many students' descriptions of their meaningful writing projects either reveal how the students themselves did this reconfiguring "to achieve their own goals" or how the faculty who assigned their projects anticipated and planned for the possibility that such reconfiguration might happen by providing some choice within their requirements. In other words, perhaps attention to learning for transfer is more important than a focus on teaching for transfer.

Others in writing studies have offered research that shows the ways in which an orientation toward teaching for transfer of writing skills may limit our understanding of what students actually do transfer in learning and writing. Consider, Susan Jarratt et al.'s (2009) "Pedagogical Memory: Writing, Mapping, Translating," which offers "an analysis of the retrospective accounts of almost a hundred student writers in their junior and senior years at a large research university" (48). Jarratt et al. set out "to discover what students remembered of their early college writing instruction and to learn more about how they chart their own paths from first-year to discipline-based writing and beyond" (66). By the conclusion of their article, the researchers offer a pedagogical approach that invites students to make their own meaning of their writing experiences and positions students as "translator[s]" with "an active relationship to pedagogical authority" so that "a student's active framing, or mapping, of writing experience across the years is valued and fostered" (66). They suggest that "rather than fixing on a set of terms and hoping they will be viable in the next context, writing teachers might place more emphasis on preparing for learning, a manner of learning that acknowledges students' pasts (rather than obliterating them with notions of progress and sophistication) and gestures toward their writing futures" (66). If "individual student's sense-making" (66) were encouraged in this way, Jarratt et al. suggest, individual students would be able to "map their own idiosyncratic pasts and to imagine future writing lives" (67). In his recent book, Guerra (2015) extends Jarratt et al.'s view:

> If there is a major difference between what they describe as pedagogical memory and what I describe as cultural modalities of memory, it is one of scope or scale. While pedagogical memory focuses on what students remember about learning to write in school, cultural modalities of memory aims for memories of a broader range of lived experiences that extend beyond the college writing classroom and out into the wider social spaces that inform their everyday lives. (64)

And he continues:

> Students need to learn to use cultural modalities of memory to highlight the rhizomatic nature of their lived experience, to wrestle with the multiple contradictions that Life in the Neither/Nor brings to light. When we constitute or reconstitute ourselves, we purposefully disrupt the need that we feel to make sense of the world in coherent and highly prescribed terms. (65)

In another recent study based on a methodology of focus groups, interviews, and interactions with students in which she asked them to "discuss their compositions in relation to one another but "did not focus [her] questions around possible domains or categories those texts might fall into" (2), Jessica Lindenman (2015), too, is able to "show that, when prompted, students invent characterization schemes for their own writing that can and do transcend the stereotypical divisions that composition scholars and teachers often impose" (3).

We see in Lindenman's (2015) work a similar path to ours; her goal is to "disrupt" the domain-based thinking about writing by offering students new kinds of questions, questions that do not force fit their thinking into domains or bounded disciplines or even into in-school or out-of-school contexts. Like Lindenman, we believe some of the geographers eager to map transfer of writing are asking students the wrong questions. Lindenman views what students have offered in answer to her questions as "idiosyncratic metageneric connections"—respecting that the formulations and connections students' make are valid and individually constructed by *them*, not by a body of research literature that imposes categories and domains. She argues for a more expansive frame (as we do next), referring to the "umbrella" of metagenres we can now believe students work under and move through with a kind of fluidity. She goes on to suggest how her findings could inform pedagogy: "If we ask students to create their own personal, flexible categories of writing, they may come to see genres as dynamic means to address repeated social exigencies, as social actions that they can adapt and re-categorize according to the work they perform" (12), and she points out that "being able to transfer writing experiences across domains first requires a student to see those experiences as connected in a meaningful way" (13). As we have described, in our study students connected their meaningful writing projects to existing passions or interests and to future writing contexts. Creating the conditions for those connections to be made is the challenge we next address.

THE MEANINGFUL WRITING PROJECT AND EXPANSIVE FRAMING

From our study and from this confirming literature, we see the need to move discussions away from a focus on teaching for transfer toward a focus on learning for transfer. While we appreciate the attention to student learning in teaching-for-transfer curricula and the research that studies those curricula, we resist the deficit orientation often in play when students are deemed lacking if their previous preparation or dispositions toward the assignment or curriculum are what prevent successful transfer. An unfortunately long tradition in higher education blames students' intransigence or their lack of willingness to learn or their seemingly stubborn hold on previously successful writing strategies, in a sense shifting responsibility from instruction and curriculum to students and labeling their "habits of mind" as the problem. We wonder, too, if a focus on teaching for transfer when prior knowledge is conceptualized in narrow ways might, ironically, disrupt any potential connections to students' passions, experiences, and identities, which our study shows are key to meaningful writing experiences.

What students told us about their most meaningful writing projects has left us thinking less about what they were taught or told about how their writing knowledge and experiences might transfer from one context to another and more about how students understood themselves as learners and writers because of the meaningful writing project itself. Reframing as *learning for transfer* removes the emphasis on transactional teaching (which, if reified, becomes a regulatory set of transfer standards, in a sense) and places the emphasis on learning, implying a more generative, reciprocal arrangement among students and teachers in which students can more fully claim their own agency and their own chosen forms of engagement. We find with Randi Engle and colleagues that "transfer is more likely to occur when learning and transfer contexts are framed *expansively* as opportunities for students to actively contribute to larger conversations that extend across times, places, people, and activities" (Engle et al. 2012, 605).

In "How Does Expansive Framing Promote Transfer?," Engle, Diane Lam, Xenia Meyer and Sarah Nix write, "Our claim is that learning and transfer contexts can be socially *framed* in different ways and that this will then influence students' propensity to transfer what they learn" (Engle et al., 2012, 217). They go on to explain:

> For example, a teacher can frame a lesson as a one-time event of learning something that students are unlikely to ever use again, or as an initial discussion of an issue that students will be actively engaging with throughout their lives. Our contention is that the first kind of framing, which we refer to as *bounded*, will tend to discourage students from later using what they learn, while the second, which we refer to as *expansive*, will tend to encourage it. (217)

Engle et al. (2012) add that "how a context is framed ends up having profound effects on whether and how its associated content knowledge is used elsewhere" and note that as "settings comprise times, places, and participants, an expansive framing of a learning setting may extend it to include the past and future, different places, and additional people" (218). They offer examples of the difference between "expansive" framing and "bounded" framing, and we are struck by how expansively framed learning encourages both the learner/writer's agency and the learner/writer's preferred way(s) of engaging with the content and the skills being learned and practiced. In other words, expansive framing potentially takes into account students' personal connection to their topics and their interests in their writing as relevant to their futures. As

Engle et al. put it, "An expansively framed learning environment may also increase the likelihood that, in a potential transfer context, students view what they learned before as having continued relevance" (221).

Also key to Engle et al.'s (2012) proposal is a sense that student authorship should be promoted. Of course, this idea of authorship resonates with us in writing studies, and those in various other fields have already employed the metaphor for a stage theory describing a process of developing self-efficacy: self-authorship (Baxter Magolda and King 2004; Fried 2016; Kegan 2000). That construct includes three components: the intrapersonal (which we see as personal connection); the interpersonal (which we see as engagement); and the cognitive (which we see as learning for transfer). Because those components of self-authorship map onto what we found, we are able to forward the idea that meaningful writing experiences contribute to the learning and development of the young adults we work with. But we believe what Engle and colleagues are saying is not metaphorical at all; their use of *authoring* applies to writing itself. They explain that when learner's "roles" (Engle et al. 2012, 218) are framed expansively, "learners are positioned as active participants in a learning context where they serve as authors of their own ideas and respondents to the ideas of others" (218). They go on to say, "This authorship role means that when students are faced with potentially new transfer problems they are ready to generate a response by adapting their existing knowledge" (225). We believe this opportunity to face "novel problems" and "adapt prior knowledge" offers some additional explanation for why so many seniors looking back on their most meaningful writing project described it as new at the time they worked on it but had become so certain it would be important or valuable or useful to them in their futures. In their meaningful writing project, they had experienced what Engle et al. call the "practice of authoring knowledge" (220). As described to us, their authorship role, which was enacted in and through their written texts, never seemed invoked just to complete one task, for merely one class or an individual professor, or even only for the grade they earned.

We believe Engle et al.'s (2012) explanation of the echoing importance of the role of authorship for expansive learning also explains some of the prevalence and power of personal connection in our study. They hypothesize that "in an expansive environment, one in which students are positioned as authors whose knowledge from prior settings is considered welcome, students are more likely to transfer-in knowledge during learning in ways that can enhance later transfer out" (224). Thus, with expansive framing, the attention is on the student and on the conditions necessary for successful learning for transfer, as well as on student agency and engagement with peers, instructors, and materials. In sum, we find strong explanatory power in the concept of expansive framing as applied to meaningful writing projects. Expanding the frame for both the entrance to an opportunity and the exit from that particular opportunity enlarges the site for students to find personal connection, imagine future selves, and immerse themselves in researching, writing, and learning content, actions vital to strengthening agency, engagement with people and materials, and learning for transfer.

TWO CASE STUDIES OF LEARNING FOR TRANSFER

As we have shown in this chapter, students' meaningful writing projects demonstrate properties of "transfer in" in terms of students' personal connection to their projects and the prior knowledge of the topic or of research and writing processes they bring to bear. The properties of "transfer forward" rest on the belief in future relevancy and future identities. In the two case studies that follow, we show a richer picture of the relationship between these students' meaningful writing projects and the concept of learning for transfer.

CASE STUDY 1—NEHA: COLLEGE HOCKEY AND THE POWER OF PERSONAL CONNECTION

Neha, a senior anthropology and international affairs dual major, identified on our survey as "Asian," "female," and "18–21." In her interview with Shelley, a sophomore English major, she describes experiences consistent with overall trends in that Neha did see her meaningful writing project as a kind of project she had not written previously and also saw it potentially connected to future writing. However, Neha's case also offers two exceptions to the overall trend of our survey findings: (1) Neha's meaningful writing experience occurred in her freshman year as opposed to an advanced disciplinary writing course or a capstone, and (2) her teacher played a fairly minimal role, at least in terms of offering direct feedback or instruction. These "outliers," in statistical speak, offer a more nuanced view of students' lived experiences with writing and reveal even more about how students use their agency and engagement, as well as their personal connection and immersed learning and writing experiences, for transfer.

Neha's meaningful writing project was, in her words, a "mini-ethnography I had to do for my Peoples and Cultures class. This was freshman year. And I was looking at hockey fan-culture." In her response to our survey, Neha described her reason for choosing this project as most meaningful: "I really enjoyed dissecting culture in various situations and combining my newfound love for hockey with anthropology." Our content analysis of that response resulted in the codes *personal connection*, *content learning*, and *affect*, and each of those elements plays a significant role in what Neha describes.

First, in terms of personal connection, here's what Neha says when Shelly asks her why she chose this project as her most meaningful one:

> My friend in my dorm, she was really into hockey, and she dragged me to this hockey game early in that semester. And I had never paid attention to sports, but she was like, "Oh, just watch it, whatever." And I thought it was really interesting to see, like, I'm sure every sport has its own rituals, but I thought it was really interesting to see the rituals that were attached to the hockey sport. Because Northeastern is a hockey school, in terms of sports, their rituals would be like, bigger and grander than any other ones. . . . So, I decided to study that, because I started to like the game, and I really wanted to analyze it though, because I was still a newcomer to it. So it was sort of, kind of like an excuse to watch more hockey. But also, it was just a really cool way to analyze what people did.

While Neha's personal connection seems at first somewhat for the sake of convenience and, simply, in the interest of seeing more hockey, later in the interview she reveals a much deeper layer of personal connection as Shelley probes further as to why Neha chose this particular project:

> That's a bit of an interesting story. It's partly because it was an anthropology project, so I wasn't an anthropology major when I took the class, and when I took the class it was just sort of like the pieces of my life fit together. Because I'm Indian and I grew up in an Indian household, but I went to school in a very white town, and it was sort of like a very American thing. I constantly had these clashing cultures. Or maybe not always clashing, but two different cultures, two different necessarily values and things and what they expected of me. It was sometimes difficult, sometime kind of cool. I always sort of felt like really conflicted about it, and I always felt like I had to side with one culture or the other. When I took the class, it sort of made me feel better about my life, and it was just sort of like, "Yes. This validates my life." In a sort of way it was like I always knew that I had, there were these two different things, but it sort of just made the lines very clear. And so that's why I switched majors. And the paper was really fun for me to write. It was also really cool for me to be able to look at the world through that anthropological lens, that I sort of already had because of living in two different cultures, kind of. It was really a fun experiment for me to do that.

Thus, for Neha, the meaningful writing project allowed her to "transfer in" and confront the tension she had lived with as a person of color growing up in a majority white community. Personal connection in this case is a powerful means of transfer between Neha's previous experiences and her meaningful writing project.

In the interviews, we asked students to talk about the processes they used to create their meaningful writing project, and we heard frequent accounts of the importance of peer review and of careful feedback from instructors. From Neha, we also hear of the use of technology, another window into how writing functions in our students' lives and how skills and strategies developed outside our classrooms might transfer to new contexts. Here's how she described her process of writing her ethnography:

> I had one of those phones that had, I think it's called Word to Go, or Documents to Go, and so I was able to put notes while I was watching the game, or during the intermission of the game, in my phone. I had a huge compilation of notes towards the end of the semester. I hadn't really done anything with them until probably two weeks before the paper was due. When it gets like the end of the semester, you always have a gazillion papers and they're all due at the same time. I had all these notes and everything that I had written about the game and then I started to craft them into a story whenever I started writing it.

As we noted, we coded Neha's survey response ("I really enjoyed dissecting culture in various situations and combining my newfound love for hockey with anthropology") *content learning* given her reference to the content of her paper. Once again, the interview amplifies that response as Neha, a senior anthropology major, describes to Shelley, a sophomore English major, the goal of writing an ethnography:

> Part of ethnography—I don't know if you're really familiar with it—part of it's like when you look at cultures, or subcultures, like hockey, or like a completely different culture, and you turn it into a narrative that explains what might be bizarre behavior, through its own eyes. So for instance . . . it can explain why certain tribes in South America use witchcraft. It's really their way of controlling, it's their way of praying to God. That kind of thing. It explains things that seem odd to us in a very basic way that makes it, like, "This isn't really so different from what we actually do, and what we do is probably bizarre to them." That's what ethnography does.

Neha also felt her ethnography would transfer forward to a degree and be useful for future writing. In her survey response, she noted, "The ethnography made me look closely at interactions between people and break them down, as well as just be more observant which is a useful skill for all writing." In her interview, she expands on this view, though she also adds a caveat:

Well, if I were to go into anthropology, then, yes, it would contribute to it in terms of ethnography. This might sound weird. I don't really anticipate doing a lot of writing in the future. I am going to be a librarian. . . . I am going to go to grad school for that in the fall. While there is going to be writing with that, I don't anticipate that any of the stuff that I have done now is going to really, like, yes, writing skills and learning how to write well will translate over, but I anticipate any writing that I have to do then is going to be very different from the stuff that I have done now.

Thus, Neha acknowledges "low-road" transfer (Perkins and Salomon 1989) of writing skills will be applicable to the writing she might do in pursuit of an MLS degree, as well as in her work as a librarian. However, she has doubts about "high-road" transfer given her expectation for "very different" writing in that work.

Finally, for this project that Neha felt was a major turning point in her academic career, helping her come to terms with her cultural identity and causing her to declare anthropology as her major, her instructor's assessment was fairly incidental to these more important outcomes. Neha told Shelley, "I got a B+ which is actually lower than I had hoped, but I still really liked it." Neha's description of her grade reminds us that faculty assessment of learning at the course level may actually have little to do with students' learning for transfer.

Overall, Neha's most meaningful writing project offers an example of the power of personal connection, in this instance a means to make sense of cultural contradictions she had lived with for a long time. Neha also valued the content she learned, as well as the method—ethnography—to discover that content. That contemporary technology not provided by the course or faculty person aided her writing processes is an acknowledgment that present generations of students might see affordances to their writing success that would surprise previous generations—and their writing instructors. While her instructor might not have specifically created this assignment with "expansive framing" in mind, the result for Neha was quite aligned with what Engle et al. (2012) describe: "In an expansive framing of roles, learners are positioned as active participants in a learning context where they serve as authors of their own ideas and respondents to the ideas of others" (218). Transfer is transformation in this case, as Neha's meaningful writing project was a starting point for her choice of major and a means to reconcile conflicting identity issues and point to meaningful writing projects as key experiences.

CASE STUDY 2—KRISTINA: MATERIALIST HISTORY AS A PASSION

Our second case study is Kristina, a senior history major and classics minor, who identified herself on our survey as "White/Caucasian," and "18–21," was interviewed by Mariana, a first-year student. Like Neha, Kristina saw her meaningful writing project as a kind of project she had not written previously, but she also saw it as potentially connected to future writing. Like 44 percent of the students in our study, Kristina wrote her meaningful writing project in her senior year, and it was also her senior capstone project. Kristina's experience, as she described it to Mariana, offers interesting details for thinking about learning for transfer: (1) Kristina says she had written many other history papers before but never a paper considering materialist history; (2) she had previously written about related content, and remembering research she hadn't been able to use in that previous paper led to the meaningful writing project; and (3) she reports how shorter, earlier papers in the class and intensive work with her professor taught her methods of material history she applied in her final project, the project she named as her meaningful writing project. Kristina is passionate about the subject matter of her project and took a class with a professor who was, in her experience, surprisingly willing to allow students to explore their own personal interests and to become very involved in their research and writing processes. Learning for transfer here involves Kristina's choice, her engagement, and her agency. But she was also passionate about and personally connected to the content she immersed herself in as she researched the project.

Asked on our survey to describe her most meaningful writing project, Kristina wrote, "I really enjoyed my capstone history paper. In this paper I was finally able to choose my topic and research something I was very interested in. I felt accomplished when I was done and knew I had done something unique." In her response to our next question, Kristina described her reason for choosing this project as most meaningful: "Made me feel accomplished and like I had done unique research." Our content analysis of that response resulted in the codes *personal connection, researching to learn,* and *accomplishment,* and each of those elements plays a significant role in what Kristina describes in her interview, especially in relation to her future goals and interests. In fact, even on the survey, Kristina offered some explanation for why she imagined she would write this way in the future: "I wrote over material history and I plan to go into museum studies so material history is an important part of the museum world."

When asked in her interview whether she'd ever written anything similar, Kristina elaborates on the newness of the task:

> I've written history papers like this, where I've had to focus on that time period, but nothing that considers material history, which I'm really interested in. I want to work in museums, and focusing on an artifact, or in this case clothing, takes more than history books and stuff. Nothing quite like this, but, yes, I've written history papers. [laughs]

Kristina's choice of topic grew from thinking and content she couldn't fit into a paper she wrote for a previous class, and her story is an important reminder that what doesn't make it into students' written projects may be as important for their learning transfer as what does make it into their texts:

> I chose clothing because I, in the past, had done for a different class assignment a paper about powdered wigs like the founding fathers wore, and when I had researched that, I found all this really interesting stuff about what clothing meant to the early Americans. It made me think, well, why don't I research that a little bit further and see what it means? That's just like personal, what I was into. We had other students in the class that did guns or cars and stuff like that. Just because of my personal interest. That's why I picked clothing, and I thought it would be interesting to look at the fashion of the time.

Listening to Kristina describe her interest in the clothing of the "founding fathers" works as a good reminder of the somewhat idiosyncratic ways students develop intellectual passion. In relation to the student participants in their research for *Engaged Writers/Dynamic Disciplines*, Thaiss and Zawacki (2006) say they were "struck again and again by these students' level of engagement in their chosen field(s)" (50), and through the Meaningful Writing Project, we, too, have been affected by what students have told us about the attention they give to their participation in disciplines and professions.

It's clear from Kristina's description of the sequencing of assignments in her class that her professor intended to give students opportunities to practice material history throughout the semester, and she intended to invite students to follow their own interests for their final project, which was begun early in the semester. The interviewer, Mariana, asks Kristina if there was any relationship between the other writing she did in this class and her meaningful writing project. Kristina answers:

> We had, I think, three short essays before this main paper, and they were all focused on material history, but it was the type of material history that the teacher chose. We did one on photographs. One on sculpture or pottery, and then one on, I think, manuscripts. Like leftover diaries or

whatever were the other ones. The same overriding topic of material history was focused on, but not clothing like I did.

The professor plays an important role in allowing every student in the class to research something the student is interested in, or to tap into *personal connection*. But from Kristina's description, a familiar theme from our study—a balance between teacher requirements and student choice (or between "bounded and "expansive" framing in Engle et al.'s (2012) terms)—clearly runs through her professor's work with students as they research and write:

> We had to stick within material history, so we had to pick some type of artifact, but after that she allowed us to take it wherever we wanted to. Whatever your interest is in, and my interest personally is revolutionary period. I really like the revolutionary war and the founding fathers and stuff, so she allowed me to do that, but then also enabled me and said, "Oh, well, if you like that, you'll like this, and why don't you look at blah, blah, blah and whatnot," and she just promoted each person's interests. Which is rare with teachers here. They want you to focus on what their interest is, but this teacher specifically allowed us to have material history as a focus, but then very different papers is what it ended up being. Like time periods, or parts of the world. The papers were from all over basically, and that's because she pushed us to do what we wanted, which was really great.

And Kristina's professor was clearly able to allow for this type of choice because her presence in the students' projects ran through the semester in ways Kristina could describe and in ways Kristina appreciated even as she pursued her own topic and research. In other words, *researching to learn* in this case was both research under the guidance of a professor and individual research.

Kristina also tells her interviewer, "I talked to a second professor, who I had had in the past, who knew this time period, but the main focus was with the professor of the class." And she notes how her small class—ten to twelve students—allowed for more interaction with her professor: "[I was] more comfortable to share my work with the other students because we were like a team. We were all working on the same type of thing. They understand where my struggle is, and I understand where theirs is."

Because Kristina's interest in researching her meaningful writing project grew from information she couldn't include in an earlier project, she had a starting point for her research and her experience writing in history:

> It's really focusing on finding sources and then compiling all my information from those sources into one complete argument. . . . With history, I've had to take other ideas and present them to prove my argument. For

me, it's been research based to prove my hypothesis I guess, if that's how you'd say it, where I'm using other peoples' evidence to support my belief instead of backing up my own belief with my own stuff.

But the excitement of this project was different, perhaps because Kristina was a senior and a self-professed "big nerd" who likes "history a lot" and who likes "the founding fathers," or perhaps because she was able to continue working on something that had interested her for a long time using new information and research, or perhaps because her project was so related to what she hoped to do in the future. Or maybe for of all of these reasons. Kristina became "really, really interested in Benjamin Franklin" but tells her interviewer, "I had never actually read his diaries or his letters. . . . Then all of a sudden, they felt real to me, instead of someone out of a history textbook." And because of that, she says, "It just made me feel, with this paper, different from all of my other papers, made me feel like I was educating somehow. Like, this is something that no one has ever written about, even though I'm sure they have." And with the agency she feels from this process, she says, "I would love to write a book about this someday just because I think it's so interesting and I haven't really been taught this in my history classes."

In sum, Kristina's learning for transfer was enabled by the personal connection she had to the topic, by the preliminary research and agency she was able to draw on from previous classes, and by the role her instructor played in sequencing a semester-long assignment and offering a balance between required components and student choice. We are also struck by how much identity is a component of this case and of so much of our survey and interview data. For Kristina, imagining herself as a historian of material culture—in the moment of her meaningful writing project, in that possible future book about Benjamin Franklin, and in her desire to work in museum studies—means transferring an identity she's gained via her meaningful writing project to a prospective identity.

We also want to make mention of the great sense of accomplishment Kristina took from this paper and from her achievement. As she told Mariana:

> Writing something that you're passionate about really, really helps for you to go on and makes it worthwhile for anyone to read and to feel proud of. I am really proud of this paper even though, at the end of the day, it is just a history paper for a class.

At the end of the day, a meaningful writing project with the potential for students to "transfer in" passion for a subject and "transfer forward" to future writing and future identities is remarkably powerful.

CONCLUSION

We have argued in this chapter for an expansive view of learning for transfer, one not merely focused on curricular or pedagogical elements that enable teaching for transfer but also on the wide range of resources, experiences, passions, and, simply, human experience students bring that offer hope for learning for transfer. We do not want to overlook the role of new opportunities in our study or the newness of the writing task as figuring strongly into why students chose it as their most meaningful. Still, the power of personal connection also provides insight into just what it was that was new for students and just what it was that was not. Opportunity seems key here given the overwhelming numbers of students who cited their meaningful writing project as an opportunity to do *something* they had not done previously (whether writing about a particular topic or exploring a new process or genre). If transfer is the invocation of prior knowledge or learning—however one describes that knowledge—the writing projects that create opportunities, allow students to connect personally in some way, and take an expansive view of learning seem most likely to result in students' meaningful experiences. These projects seem to us to be holistic—not merely about content or genre or process but also about mind and body, heart and head—and to act as a kind of mirror in which students can see their pasts and futures, enabling them to map those on to their writing projects to make meaning.

Of course, learning and teaching are intertwined, and in the next chapter we focus on what we learned from faculty who were named by students as having taught the class in which their meaningful writing projects occurred. We show that the projects themselves can be thought of as spaces in which student and faculty values and goals for writing meet (and, at times, clash), spaces in which student agency, engagement, and learning for transfer play key roles.

5

MEANINGFUL WRITING
HAPPENS WHEN . . .

In the previous three chapters we relied on student-survey and interview data to characterize the meaning students derive from their writing. More specifically, we explored the way meaningful writing projects offer opportunities for

- student agency;
- engagement with instructors, peers, and materials (particularly the content learned in the development of the project);
- learning that connects to previous experiences and passions and to future aspirations and identities.

When we considered how and where meaningful writing projects originated, we found that 94 percent of the seniors who participated in our survey indicated that their meaningful writing projects were written as a course assignment. We were surprised by this finding. Our expectation was that at Northeastern, in particular, given the strong presence and popularity of six-month full-time "co-op" work experiences students often cite as the key influence of their undergraduate careers, out-of-class writing would be named more frequently. However, the percentage of course assignments named as meaningful writing projects at Northeastern was even higher than the average, encompassing nearly 96 percent of all responses. As we point out in chapter 3 about engagement, from students' perspectives, faculty had varying degrees of influence on meaningful writing projects. But it is clear that instructors in these courses were doing something to cultivate the meaning students derived from their writing projects, and we hoped our research would shed light on those practices. What remains consistent across the meaningful writing projects appears to be a set of opportunities offered by faculty. Projects deemed meaningful by over seven hundred students invite them to

- tap into the power of personal connection;
- see what they're writing as applicable, relevant, real world, and connected to their future selves;

DOI: 10.7330/9781607325802.c005

- immerse themselves in what they're thinking, writing, and researching, including engagement in processes of writing.

In other words, potentially any project in any course, in any program, department, or discipline—whether the course is or isn't designated writing intensive—can become a meaningful writing project with the right (for that moment) combination of these opportunities.

In this chapter, we rely on faculty perspectives to describe these elements of meaningful writing projects, triangulating faculty accounts with what students told us they value. Our findings from the faculty survey and interviews describe the contours of shared learning places in rich ways we could not see from student data alone. In short, we highlight what students and faculty agree are the elements of meaningful writing projects, elements we hope might be replicated in every setting—if not for every assignment.

FACULTY DESCRIBE "WHY MEANINGFUL?"

While our initial intent was to conduct follow-up interviews with faculty named as having taught courses in which the meaningful writing project took place (and we had IRB approval to do so), we expected the same few faculty to be named repeatedly. In other words, despite our decades of collective experience working with faculty at many universities, we assumed that *experiencing* a meaningful writing project would be a relatively isolated phenomenon. However, we were (happily) wrong. In fact, we were delighted that students identified nearly five hundred faculty across our three institutions, most named only once. We wondered what we might learn from these faculty about the design of their particular assignments that led to meaningful writing and how they incorporated writing into their teaching. To that end we designed a survey to address these questions, and, as we point out in chapter 1, received 160 faculty responses. Further, in interviews with sixty of those faculty, our undergraduate researchers asked about the evolution of those assignments, about faculty members' own meaningful writing, and about the larger role of writing in their teaching.

As we also describe in chapter 1, our first of two faculty survey questions was "We're sending you this survey because a student named a writing project written for your course as the most meaningful of their undergraduate career. Why do think that was so?" To be consistent with our intent to understand students' perspectives of their meaningful writing experiences, we analyzed faculty's responses to this question with the same codes (see app. F) that emerged from students'

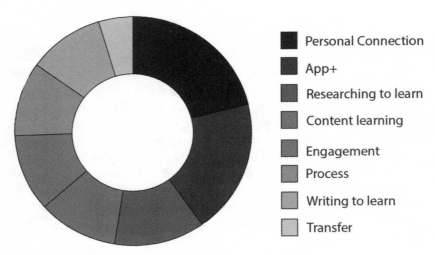

Figure 5.1. Faculty survey question 1: most frequent codes.

responses to the question of why the project they chose was meaning-ful (and, as was true for our analysis of student data, we collaboratively conducted this coding). Our aim was to use the lens of student mean-ingfulness to understand what faculty were telling us about those same assignments.

Figure 5.1 shows the most frequent codes from the faculty surveys. As was true for the coding of students' descriptions of why the project was meaningful, the most frequent response was to note a *personal con-nection* (occurring in 41 percent of all responses) or that the project was relevant to students and applicable to their futures (*app+* occurring in 37 percent of all responses). After *personal connection* and *app+*, several codes occurred in relatively similar numbers. Specifically, we coded these responses as *researching to learn* (occurring in 23 percent of all responses), *content learning* (21 percent), *engagement* (21 percent), *pro-cess* (20 percent), and *writing to learn* (20 percent). Put another way, as was true for students, faculty understand meaningful writing projects as ones in which students had opportunities to make a personal connec-tion to what they were writing, see the task as relevant/authentic/appli-cable, and immerse themselves in processes of writing and researching to learn content.

In terms of how student and faculty responses to "Why meaning-ful?" compared, as shown in figure 5.2, we did see some interesting differences between the two groups in which codes occurred most fre-quently. Specifically, faculty were much more likely to name "audience,"

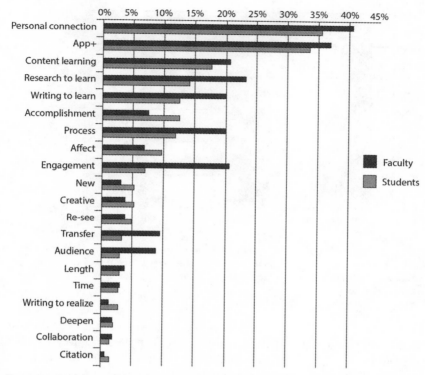

Figure 5.2. Students' writing/faculty assignments: "Why meaningful?" compared.

"transfer," "writing to learn," "researching to learn," "process," and "engagement" than were students (and all of these differences are statistically significant at p < .05).

Perhaps these findings are not a surprise, as all these components tend to be behind-the-curtain practices of many of our writing assignments. Consider even our most common intentions and transparent activities, say, when we specify a particular audience, establish the goal to bring together previous learning, describe the process students will use to compose, and engage in one-on-one conferencing with students. Faculty might be building those practices in, but the fact of them is not necessarily what students point to as making the project most meaningful. And not surprisingly, students were more likely to name accomplishment as a reason the writing project was meaningful, given that accomplishing the task might be more tied to student experience than to faculty intent. It is important to reiterate, however, that what we coded *personal connection* and *app+* figure prominently for both

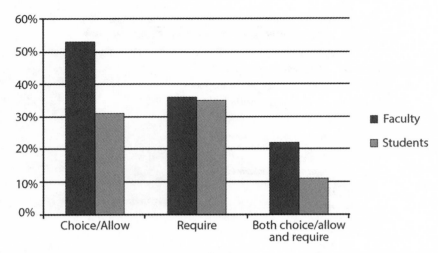

Figure 5.3. Percentage of student and faculty survey responses indicating assignment allowed choice and/or had required elements. (Differences between student and faculty occurrences of choice/allow and occurrences of both choice/allow and require are significant at p < 0.05.)

faculty and students as the two most frequent reasons the writing project was meaningful. The ways assignments offered space for students' passions, interests, and experiences and the connection between those assignments and students' future curricular and professional lives are quite powerful.

As we describe in chapter 2 on agency, one element we saw repeatedly in student-survey responses was whether the assignment or the instructor offered students opportunities for exploration or allowed for some sort of freedom. This choice/allow component was often balanced by a description of required elements. Faculty, similarly, included in their descriptions of assignments notions of choice/allow and require. The frequency with which we saw the element of choice/allow, however, differed between student and faculty responses, as shown in figure 5.3. Faculty were much more likely than students to name an assignment as giving students choice or saying it allowed students room to maneuver. In faculty responses, we also saw *require* and *allow* co-occurring twice as frequently as in students' responses. However, both faculty and students named *required* at a similar rate.

In several survey responses, faculty attempted to describe that sweet spot between giving students freedom to explore yet offering enough structure for students to succeed:

- I try to come up with writing assignments that are open-ended enough to allow students to explore things that interest them, yet are guided enough that the students don't get lost in choice.

- I believe the project was meaningful to the student because it honestly attempted to allow for as much freedom and self-direction as possible while still providing parameters necessary for focus and communication.

- While it is very structured, [the assignment] allows the student to tap into their altruistic passions to change their world.

- I don't assign topics to the students, but look to support topics they are passionate about. This freedom can be a huge burden to some students, but it also provides an opportunity for students to consider a topic that really interests them—one that they want to explore/know more about/question.

Overall, faculty responses to the question of why they believed a student chose an assignment as leading to meaningful writing offer a variety of elements that range across fields, disciplines, and the tasks themselves: in the view of faculty in our study, meaningful writing assignments offer opportunities for students to tap into passions and interests, to engage in writing and research processes that enable them to learn course content, and to see applicability to future writing or future careers. Faculty named for assigning meaningful writing projects also tried to strike a balance between required elements and student autonomy. That students also see these qualities as important—though not always in the same measure as faculty—is more evidence of their impact.

CASE STUDIES OF WHEN MEANINGFUL WRITING HAPPENS—FOR STUDENTS AND FACULTY

In what follows, we offer several in-depth examples of the triangulation of what students described in surveys and interviews as reasons they chose a writing project as meaningful and what faculty across a range of disciplines and in courses large and small told our undergraduate researchers about the behind-the-curtain details of their assignments. We attempt to capture the multidimensionality of meaningful writing projects, showing how students' and instructors' values and beliefs about writing come together—and at times clash—in those projects named as most meaningful. Chris Gallagher (2002) defines "pedagogy" as "what happens when people seek to produce knowledge together" (xvi). We believe the pedagogy that produces meaningful writing projects is that sort of collaborative, knowledge-making effort. Once again, the meaningful writing project is a meeting space, one in which student agency, engagement, and learning for transfer are possible, enabled by the extent to which personal connection, applicability, and immersion in processes of researching, writing, and thinking might occur.

We need to note that not all of these elements were in play for any single assignment; thus, we are not necessarily concluding that all writing assignments must include each element. Instead, what we saw was that deliberate assignment design—and faculty values and goals about teaching with writing more generally—included these elements where appropriate. The cases that follow highlight several of those appropriate moments.

A THEOLOGIAN VALUES REFLECTION IN FIRST-YEAR WRITING

The senior who cited this first-year course wrote on her survey, "The attack of September 11 really affected me and to reflect about the new WTC seems to be the most meaningful in all of the papers i wrote for classes." She added that she hoped to do this type of writing again when she went on to "work for US Embassy as a Foreign Officer for foreign diplomacy," a profession she clearly imagined would include contemplation and/or deliberation. Here, personal connection to the meaningful writing project comes from a student's significant experience when she was quite young but doesn't map to her future as exactly as one might expect.

When Lydia, a theology professor, submitted her faculty survey and responded to our question about why she thought a student had found her assignment meaningful, she wrote, "'Preservation' was the theme of that course, and the final reflection that semester was assessing and reflecting on the designs proposed for the World Trade Center site. Perhaps the student found this to be most relevant to his or her learning and experience." In fact, it does not come as a surprise to us that a theologian—someone with meditative, reflective, and questioning disciplinary education and experiences—would value reflection in students' writing, but it is interesting to hear the way Lydia describes her commitment to a variety of types of reflection in writing, learning, and teaching to her undergraduate interviewer. For example, she describes taking students on a field trip to prepare them for academic service learning:

> What's particularly satisfying is that's the only way I can figure out what students are thinking or absorbing or how they're interacting; it's amazing. I took the freshmen to St. X Church. They all had to do field work. It was in local parishes, and they're not Catholic. I wanted them to know what was inside a church and to feel comfortable. We went over there. They

wanted to be out. But when I read the reflection papers, they were awesome. All the stuff going on inside of them, I wouldn't have a clue about. Professors who don't encourage writing, I don't know how they ever know what's inside the students.

Connecting via written reflection to "what's inside the students" is key for this faculty member. She also describes how and why she values a required midsemester reflection:

I do a kind of midcourse correction. It's not so much a test as it is, how is it going? How are you doing? What can I help you with? What do you think about where are you in your research paper? Where are you with this? Where are you with that? It's kind of a plea to conscience or something. But to me too, so if they tell me what's going well and what's not going well, I'll change course too.

Lydia is actually able to tell her interviewer quite explicitly what she hopes students will accomplish. She says, "I value depth of reflection more than surface information." Reflection as an essential means of learning is well known (e.g., Yancey 1998); however, in this case, reflection is a means of having students connect with topics of their writing and provides a window for faculty engagement to better understand those connections is quite powerful. The student acquires a kind of agency, and the meaningful writing project is a space inhabited by student and faculty in the interest of better engaging with course content. And the course content and reflection and writing process becomes, in the context of the meaningful writing project, important to how the student imagines their future.

A DANCE TEACHER BRINGS BODY AND BRAIN TOGETHER

Reflection was also key to a dance student who told us her meaningful writing project gave her insight into the practices of dance and of the use of writing to better understand those practices. As the student noted in her survey response, her meaningful writing project was "writing about a specific choreographer for dance styles. Since I don't write papers often, this paper was in a subject I am interested in. Also it opened my eyes up to how important research can be in my field of study." This engagement with the content and genres of her field and the variety of ways to explore that content also played a role in what the student saw as connection to her future writing (however reluctantly): "I don't want to write. However if I do it will be choreography so seeing the excerpts of notes from choreographers gave me insight into how some write notes."

Her experienced dance professor, Olive, designs writing assignments to give dance majors the opportunity to move through a series of realizations. Her beliefs about the importance of reflective writing are apparent in her assignments; students' dance moves are filmed, after which they are asked to respond to the videos:

> I do some videotaping and then let them observe it and say, "Okay, what do you see? Write down what you see you need to work on. Write down how you feel about where you've improved, where you need to improve."

Further, Olive believes the embodied nature of dance can be transformed into self-awareness or a different aspect of personal connection, via writing:

> Sometimes, by the students writing it down, it gets in their head because dancers are visual and ear. They learn completely different than everybody else. I like to make to make them write so that I see what's really going on in their head, not just their bodies.

> It all comes together because dancers have to use their brain, and they tend to be more physical. I always appreciate dancers who think, and think outside their dancing, instead of being a bun head. When they wear their little buns, we call them bun heads. You want the ones who have an open mind, really open their brain to other things in their lives besides just dance, because you don't know where your life's going to take you.

Olive shares her beliefs not only about the mediating impact of writing in a performance art but also her beliefs about what (and how) dancers need to be thinking and writing about for their futures. For student and instructor in this case, personal connection is inseparable from successful performance, whether in writing or in dance.

A BIOLOGIST TEACHES A GENETICS LABORATORY COURSE

The writing students see as relevant or applicable is often apparent in STEM fields in which students plan on careers in health, medicine, or engineering and are engaging in communicative practices modeled on those they will engage in postgraduation. In the case that follows, however, the faculty member sees the task as not merely instrumental but as central to the need for scientists to communicate with technical and nontechnical readers and advocate for the work they do.

The student in this case is a business administration major with intentions of applying to medical school. He cited as most meaningful a genetics lab class, which he took as a senior:

The most meaningful piece of writing that I believe I have done is probably writing case studies for my genetics and microbiology lab. This was meaningful to me because I will be able to use these skills in medical school. The project that I have in mind was an experiment on the fruit fly and how they reproduce genetically.

In addition to the reasons he offered above, this student added, "The fact that I will use these skills in medical school made it meaningful to me." Thus, the relevance and applicability of this project, along with the opportunity to learn scientific content, are what made it meaningful.

The faculty member in this case, Ellen, an associate professor of biology, is deliberate about this relevance in this lab assignment, one that's been long standing in her course, which has a lecture component for all two hundred students and a lab component in which students are working in groups of no more than eighteen. Ellen describes this ten-to-twelve-page report as akin to a professional genre or based on the "model [of] how a scientific paper is written. The students write an abstract, an introduction, a description of their methods that they use for the experiment. The results . . . there's a statistical analysis of the product that they did. Then, they write a short discussion section about what was meaningful about what the experiment's shown."

Ellen's beliefs about student writing and about this project and its importance come through after her interviewer asks if Ellen might ever want change anything about it:

> I keep doing it because it's really hard to change. It's really valuable. The more practice people get at writing in the discipline, the better they'll be at it. It's a difficult new skill to learn. Scientific writing has its own rules. It's not really like writing that most people learn in high school, unless somebody's specialized in that. It's not like writing an essay.
>
> People come in with an essay-writing style. It's not the style that we're trying to teach them to do. They do need to do it. They need practice. I find for myself, as professional writing, the writing helps me, actually, organize my thoughts. Actually, writing it helps me think about the experiment in a much deeper way than any other way.
>
> I think that's very important. I wouldn't change the writing assignment at all. I might change what the experiment actually was. In the experiment, they follow along like a cookbook. In the experiment, there's not really an experiment. It is an experiment, but everyone's doing the same thing, and we know what the right answer is, which is not science.

Later in the interview, Ellen offers an additional reason this fairly common writing task in the sciences is one she feels is so valuable, attesting to its applicability in more ways than might have first been apparent:

One of the most important things to learn as a scientist, and most scientists are probably terrible at it, is communicating what's important about the science to somebody that's not a scientist or is not in the field. I think society in general doesn't value science nearly as much as they need to for civilization to continue. [laughs] That's partially our fault. We don't tell them what we're doing, what's cool about it, and what's important about it, and why we do it. That's this crazy stereotype about what scientists are like and what we're doing. That's our fault because we can't communicate to people.

Thus, the progression from experimental research to communicating that research both to scientific and nonscientific audiences is vital, in Ellen's view. While the routine task of a laboratory report might seem mundane to students, the ways in which this task might serve as a vehicle of discovery, creativity, and professional preparation offer a meaningful writing project applicable in a very broad sense. Deliberately designed for this applicability, the assignment offers the student and Ellen an opportunity to create a learning space for the student to be and to communicate as a scientist.

AN ACCOUNTING PROFESSOR TEACHES AUDITING

Two different students cited the audit report they wrote for a college of business class as their most meaningful. The first, an accounting major, took the class as a junior and described his most meaningful writing project: "I had to write an audit report for a company I was assigned. I had to analyze the company, and outline the risks, and what audit procedures I saw necessary. It was a very extensive and in depth paper, with a page requirement of 30 pages." For why he chose this project as most meaningful, he responded, "It is directly related to my career aspirations. It brought together all of the course concepts and made us apply them in a very realistic way."

The second student was also an accounting major and also took the course in his junior year (though in a different semester than the first student). He described his meaningful writing project: "We had to essentially do a mock audit of a Company based on their financial statements. To do this I evaluated the risks they have based on their industry and their financial ratios. In cost accounting I made up a business, set up a costing system for it, predicted costs, and made a 3 year budget for the business." As to why it was most meaningful, this student wrote, "[It was] all inclusive of things I had learned in [the class]. [It was] challenging and I was proud of the work that I did. I really learned to apply the concepts we studied instead of just being tested on them."

Application, accomplishment, and relevance are all factors the instructor, Walter, an assistant teaching professor of accounting, deliberately builds into his assignment—and how he teaches and assesses it—based on the kinds of work he knows his students will need to do after graduation. For Walter, the key aspect of this assignment is the focus on immersion in processes rather than attention to outcomes:

> My students told me, "I have never thought so hard about any project." It's not the writing. The writing is the derivative. That just happens to be the outcome. It's not the writing assignment in and of itself. It's the process that they have to go through to create that outcome.
>
> It's the process that's the most important because it's that thinking process, that thought process, that "OK, I've got to understand the business. How do I do that? Where do I get the information? What should go in there?" By making those very simple statements, understand the business? The student now has to ask lots of questions that I do not give answers to.

Walter's distrust of outcomes is tied to what he sees as most important for students in his class and in their careers: the need to have the tools to tackle unstructured problems and focus on processes:

> Outcomes are not reproducible, especially when you're dealing with something that's this unstructured. Processes, thought processes, thinking processes, the how, those are reproducible to other areas, other things that they will do in their life.
>
> The writing is not the most relevant thing. The writing again is just the outcome. I don't care about the writing. Again, outcomes are uninteresting to me. They just happen to be demonstrations of the process that the student went through, and that's it. It's a documentation of process.
>
> Now, I have students coming to me and going, "I wish your class was still going on. . . . That was the most meaningful thing that I did." It has nothing to do with the writing. It has everything to do with the process that they're going through.

When Walter's interviewer, Jan, a first-year English major, asks Walter if he was surprised that students chose this assignment as most meaningful, he responds with

> unsurprised. Because I know it's a meaningful writing assignment. It's not very surprising that it would be because it is probably . . . I like to think that when I design a course that my courses are the hardest courses in the business school. Anything that a student takes in my course is going to probably be one of the most meaningful things that they ever do in their life. Whether or not that's true or not, I don't care. I don't care.
>
> But shouldn't we all be trying to shoot for that level of engagement? That level of complexity? Trying to challenge these young, bright minds and

pushing them as hard as we possibly can. I think that's what we all should try to be doing; that's what I try to do.

Walter's goal to engage his students in the processes of thinking and writing auditors need to learn and do—essentially to develop agency as auditors to tackle unstructured problems and to use writing as a tool for learning and for communicating that learning—did not strike us as radical or unusual, despite his, at times, strident tone. If anything, we found Walter's honesty and candor refreshing; clearly, many of his students do, too.

A PHARMACEUTICAL SCIENTIST MENTORS A SENIOR THESIS WRITER

Immersion in thinking, writing, and research processes is often characteristic of capstone experiences, which figured prominently in our student-survey data. In this case, the project shared those immersive qualities with capstone projects but took place as part of an independent study the student conducted with a faculty member in the Department of Pharmaceutical Sciences. Because of that context, the faculty member knew (and remembered fondly) the student once she saw the description of the project. However, the intensity of this project—the engagement between faculty and student and the ways in which the student developed agency as an independent researcher—were potential barriers to scaling up such experiences and offer a cautionary tale as to how immersive meaningful writing projects such as this one might be relatively rare.

Here's how that student, a pharmacy major and business administration minor, described her project:

> My most meaningful project was my Junior/Senior Honors project. I work in a pharmaceutical sciences lab with a professor who teaches one of my pharmacy courses. My project combines pharmacy and pharmaceutical sciences, making it a more unique experience than had I focused on just pharmacy like my classmates. I learned to write like a scientist while learning new concepts at the same time.

For why this project was meaningful, she added, "It was a self-created project that I worked hard with a professor to earn and gained a lot of experience doing research as well as writing skills."

The student's goals to combine two areas of interest—the practical side of pharmacy and the research side of pharmaceutical sciences—and to learn to "write like a scientist" are quite aligned with what Gaby, a first-year English major, found in her interview with Brenda, the instructor. For Brenda, however, shaping this experience involves her goal of mutual learning:

> Ultimately, what you want is that the student is going to not just read the basic material in the field and be able to give you back what you already know, but they're going to go beyond what you already know. They're going to teach you about the field because they're going to be reading things and understanding it in a different way than you do.

> Seeing things, because it's a big world, that you never saw. Connections that you didn't realize. Ultimately, what starts out as they're very dependent and they don't know much at all about what they're working on, they become the experts, and then they teach you what you should know. That's really the most fun part of it.

Brenda also tells Gaby that when deciding with whom to work on a senior thesis, she needs to be choosy because of her goal of making this relationship so intense: "It's a connection that's really very personal between me and that person. Most people I turn down because I just don't feel that connection."

When Gaby learns of this intensity of this relationship, she follows up by asking how it extends to Brenda's additional teaching:

> GABY: It seems a lot like a two-way street if you have to spend so much time with the student one-on-one.
>
> BRENDA: Yeah.
>
> GABY: Have these projects, these senior theses, influenced your use of writing in your other classes in any way?
>
> BRENDA: Yes, it has. It's made me not want to do writing in my other classes because it's too hard. I'm investing myself in this thesis writing thing, scientific writing about my research, because I realize how hard this is. I can't possibly take on having 150 pharmacy students, going into whether they're writing clearly, whether they really explained it well, whether they got it right.

Brenda's goals for students' writing—and her frustration in achieving those goals—also extend to the PhD students she works with:

> When I do that with a longer document and a PhD student who's trying to graduate in May and they're not done, and I'm holding them back because it's not written well yet, it still has flaws, you still didn't explain this well, your data still doesn't look right, then they get thinking that it's abuse, that I'm just picking on them, insisting that they have this perfect document when good enough is good enough. That's where it starts getting difficult.

Thus, Brenda's goal for a well-written thesis, whether from a senior or from a PhD student, is one she feels is not always aligned with students' goals, whether that's to graduate or to move on to the next project. This conflict is not unusual in our experience, but it speaks to the ways faculty like Brenda might be supported in their practices. Brenda herself speaks to this need for support near the end of her interview with Gaby as she asks Gaby about her experiences tutoring in the writing center:

> But I'd like to know if the writing center, you and your colleagues there . . . could help me learn to do it better. Is there a shortcut to working one-on-one with somebody hour after hour after hour like this? How do other people do it? Maybe it's easier, and I just haven't figured out yet how.

Brenda would like to expand her repertoire of practices, be more efficient with her time, and have an impact on a great number of students—in other words, cultivate more meaningful writing projects. These do not strike us as unusual goals for faculty across the university; achieving them in the conditions of large numbers of students and defined semesters is a different matter.

A WRITING PROGRAM INSTRUCTOR TEACHES ADVANCED WRITING IN THE HEALTH SCIENCES

The student in this case, a behavioral neuroscience major, took her advanced writing in the health sciences course as a senior and described her project in our survey as "a research paper on prescription drug abuse among teens in the United States." In answering the question about why it was most meaningful, she wrote, "It allowed me to learn more about the subject and use this information in the future to help my patients as a health care provider." While the student reported she had not written anything like this previously, she also did not anticipate having to write similar projects in the future, adding that "as a healthcare provider, I will not be writing research papers. However, it did help me to learn about an important subject in my field." Thus, this project was applicable to her future, offered an opportunity to learn content, and allowed her to be immersed in research and writing practices.

The instructor in this case, Maura, a full-time lecturer in the writing program, is deliberate in designing these opportunities for her students, ones that come from her expertise as an experienced writing instructor and as a published and active author on healthcare issues.

Maura describes to the undergraduate conducting the interview two particular activities she's embedded in the course—the practice of revision and feedback and her practice of assessment—and how each of these practices is designed to fit students' needs. She admits, however, that her practice of assessment might be at odds with students' grade expectations.

In terms of revision and feedback, Maura describes the features of her approach:

> We always start off with a brainstorming. I say, before we read the prompt or anything, "Let's talk about what you know about public writing." What are the purposes? What are the characteristics? Where do you see it most?" Then we work through the assignment prompt, answer all those rudimentary questions.
>
> I also do a lot with samples before they ever draft anything. We look at rough drafts of previous semesters, as a class, and do miniworkshops, and say, "What's working really well here? What might we extrapolate, but what would you tell this writer if you were that peer reviewer? What do you think they could benefit from?"
>
> Then they draft, they do class-wide workshops of volunteers, and then we do small-group peer reviews. There's always at least a week between when they get my comments back and the final. We do in-class writing consults, where I say, "We have half an hour. Those of you with more specific questions, let's talk one on one."
>
> It took a while to get comfortable to actually use some of that class time in that way, but it really makes a lot of sense because we're there, we're thinking about revising, and we're doing the work together there.
>
> I teach a lot of online classes, too, so it's a totally separate process. We do a lot with models, too, certainly, but it is a lot different than how we open up each unit in person. . . . There's always a draft, there are always workshops, there's always peer review. There's always time to come meet with me.

Given the collaborative nature of this composing process, whether students are collaborating with each other or with Maura, when it comes to assessment, Maura describes practices that balance health science students' high expectations for themselves and her commitment to collaboration and transparency:

> I have individual rubrics, custom rubrics, for every unit. They're holistic, so that encompasses their peer reviews, too. They're very detailed rubrics, but there's also room for me to write a comment in every field, and then room for me to write overall comments at the end.
>
> I really try, especially because I know that the students who don't get grades that they're used to getting are going to want to know why, why, why. Sometimes students are very hard on themselves. . . . I get that. I respect that. I tend to write more to the students who aren't getting the A's and A-'s. I don't feel like I need to write pages to say, "This is wonder-

ful. You get an A." I really do try to say, "I see a lot of progress here, and I really like what you've done from the draft. Moving forward, I still think we need to work a little bit more on transitions," for example.

I do approach grading . . . I try to be objective because I know that reading essays is subjective. I try to have my feedback be as transparent, clear, and comprehensive, as possible.

While Maura's practices might be familiar to readers with solid grounding in writing-process pedagogy, we highlight them here because of the ways she describes those practices while simultaneously stressing the qualities of meaningful writing our research consistently points to: students' personal connection to the content, development of expertise in the genres of their disciplines, and application of their school-based project to the writing they might do after graduation.

A PSYCHOLOGY PROFESSOR TEACHES
RESEARCH METHODS WITH A TEAM

Unlike many of the projects we heard about in our research, this particular one occurred in a large class; however, like the previous one, it involved immersion in the practices of writing, researching, and collaboration. One of two students who said this was their most meaningful writing project, a psychology major, described the practices as she had experienced them:

During my senior year fall semester, I had to write a psychological research paper. This was my first time writing such a paper in APA format about a study I researched and wrote about as if I had conducted it. The reason why it was so meaningful was because the class was based in a way where I had to write five drafts of this paper, and each time I received feedback about to what to fix, what was wrong, etc. It was very time consuming and stressful, but it was a great learning experience for future assignments.

As the instructor, Staci, noted in the interview, "I'm a lead professor . . . and I'm responsible for the design of the class and implementation of class, but there's four labs. The cap, it's varied between . . . it used to be sixty and it moved up to one hundred. Now it's about eighty-eight, I think is the cap, depending upon the room that we're in."

Asked on the faculty survey why she felt multiple students had cited the psychology methods class she teaches with a team of graduate students, Staci, an experienced clinician and researcher, said:

I think they may have valued the experience because we provide a great deal of support and direction. I also think the assignment requires rigorous scholarly thinking plus creativity. The assignment is structured, and they work collaboratively with their lab instructors and their classmates. The task requires them to read a great deal of scientific literature and to develop a research plan. As a consequence, they have the opportunity to structure their thinking but also add new ideas.

In her interview, Staci described how she and her team continually revise the assignment: "I've actually been doing this for almost twenty years, although modifications have been made many, many, many times. We actually take the students' comments, either directly in the class or in the classroom evaluations, to help us modify it better. To help us understand more what they need." In this way, practices are informed by students' experiences and not just by faculty goals. The practices themselves also support the students as they do the work. As Staci explained to her interviewer, "It's a mastery grade with very, very clear rubrics, so we get a lot of A's because people know exactly what they're supposed to . . . it's a very hard course. It's what the student said, 'It's a very hard course but I can do it.'" Interestingly, Staci has even imagined how those students who fail the course become participants in the course's practices when they retake the course. "There are people . . . not many, but there's always a proportion of students who fail and will come back to visit us two or three times until they can get it. We're happy to see them and they often become team leaders."

As is true for many of the assignments we heard about, the research-methods sequence has both required elements and choice: "We give them a general topic and one review paper, but then they have to go find their other empirical papers on their own. They get help to do it, and they can do it with their classmates, but the actual research papers, they have to search." Staci and her team also use peer review and modeling. "It's so hard that we break it down into small pieces, and we have them write each small piece, go over it publicly in class with other people, like with their essays on the board. Then they get feedback from their teaching instructors. Then they go on to the next step, and they pull the whole thing together."

Immersing students in the practices of drafting and revision are familiar in process pedagogy; however, requiring students to engage in these practices in a course for majors with eighty-eight students and having a student identify the project for that class as most meaningful because of these immersive practices are what impress us here. Staci very deliberately and quite successfully creates the conditions for meaningful writing to happen. And while the research experience might not be as full as it might be in a capstone or in a collaborative lab, for example, as the other student who identified the project in this class as most meaningful, a social work major, wrote on the survey, "It taught me how real research is [done] and how to write a paper on the process."

AN ADJUNCT INSTRUCTOR TEACHES LITERATURE ONLINE

In this case, a meaningful writing project emerged from the nontraditional locations of both instructor and student, and it is particularly marked by the personal connection both bring to the task, as well by the opportunities for content learning. Will is an adjunct instructor in a college of liberal studies known for its online courses for nontraditional, returning, and distance students. Will's life is bookended by his own meaningful writing experiences. When asked by our researcher to describe his most meaningful writing project as an undergraduate, he said:

> Wow, man, you have me going back a ways here. Holy mackerel, I've got to think about this for a while. . . . I know, I think. I took a course as an undergraduate in creative nonfiction. I had never done that sort of writing before. It was very difficult, extremely difficult, for me to lay it all out there, which you have to do when you write essays. . . . I struggled very hard with that. I culminated it with an essay I wrote on my experiences as an infantryman in Vietnam. . . . I made the turn with that particular essay. I felt really, really good about having been able to do that.

When asked about his current writing, Will lit up with excitement:

> What I write about is what I'm interested in, and what I'm interested in, one of my passions, is falconry. I'm a falconer, so I've been doing a lot of writing on that, essays and also I've written three little books on falconry.

The strong personal connection Will feels with his past and current writing projects figures prominently in the goals and values he builds into his own students' tasks. He stated, "What I have found is that we do our best and students do their best in terms of writing when they're writing on a topic they're particularly interested in." This belief is consistent with the goals for the course; while not overtly inviting personal connections through the assignment prompts, we see an effective setup for intensive engagement with content.

In accord with this goal, the student who named this class and project as most meaningful—an over-thirty-year-old returning student—discovered a personal connection or something he was really interested in. Engaging with that content was transformative for him: "The significance of this assignment to me was that I gained a heightened appreciation for the values and philosophies of natives and pioneers of the United States throughout the twentieth century."

There is, however, a caveat to meaningfulness the student mentions in both his initial survey answer and in more detail during an interview. Apparently, he could not comply perfectly with MLA documentation (having been familiar with APA) and believed his B grade for the assignment was due to that struggle. When asked to talk about the process of writing his project, the student launched directly into this issue:

> I'm used to writing APA. I got graded pretty heavily against my paper because it was an MLA format that was required in the class. No matter what, I just apparently wasn't able to conform to the professor's style requirements. . . . I got a B. It was the formatting totally! He even made a note in grading it that effectively I didn't want to conform to his style, and it wasn't like some kind of anarchist attitude or anything. It was just an inability to satisfy his desire. I guess I didn't know what he was asking of me, and it was rather frustrating.

Will did not recall this particular student or his own demand for correct documentation style but described his general feelings about grading in his course, an online elective designed specifically for nonmajors and returning adult students:

> Unfortunately, I have found that most of the students are not good writers. That was frustrating, but, realizing this, I did not grade them on grammar, punctuation, spelling, and all that sort of stuff. I just didn't do it because I just didn't think it was right. . . . What I looked at was content and organization. If they had it organized nicely and the content, that is what I really graded them on.

We are sure the student would disagree with Will's purported fair evaluation practices; as he wrote in the "add additional comments" text box on our survey, "The professor did not like my writing style." Even the undergraduate researcher, in her postinterview reflection, noted that "it seemed like the most frustrating aspect to him was the professor focused too much on style rather than content."

But it was the content that did not disappoint. In an interview, the student told stories he learned in reading literature of the American West: "It's fantastic literature. I would actually want to spend more time. Take another course, another degree program. Sign me up! . . . It was inspiring. It was absolutely the stories." As a senior working on a BS degree in natural sciences, he was moved by an Amy Tan story in the course anthology and "ran to the library" to find *The Joy Luck Club*: "I read it. The whole book. She's an incredible writer. She spoke at the museum, and I took my textbook with me and I got her autograph. I had her sign that chapter in the book."

While the student and instructor never met face to face, and he referred to Will only as "he" and only mentioned him in the context of the documentation-style demands, the student seems to have had a rich experience with the material and found the writing assignments clear and open enough that he could explore this new literature even more deeply by writing about it. Personal connection and content learning were quite powerful here, connecting teacher and student in a meaningful learning experience, despite a lack of alignment over assessment criteria.

CONCLUSION

In this chapter, we have focused on faculty perspectives, learning from a diverse range of faculty how personal connection, applicability, and immersion in processes of thinking and writing are central to the tasks students told us led to meaningful writing:

- A theology professor teaching a first-year seminar builds in reflection on content and on personal connection.
- A dance teacher designs assignments for dance majors to use writing as a way to express the physical.
- A biologist asks students in a genetics laboratory course to write to learn content and professional genres and to communicate to the larger public.
- An accounting professor teaches auditing as a process, one in which students connect to their futures when the written processes of problem solving are most valued.
- A pharmaceutical science professor conducts a writing-intensive independent study with a student, immersing her in the research and writing practices of her field.
- A writing program instructor engages health science students in researching, writing, and collaboration, drawing connections to content and to students' futures.
- A psychology professor immerses students in research, writing, and peer-review practices appropriate to her field, despite the constraints of a large class.
- An adjunct English instructor teaches an online literature course to returning adults and creates meaningful connections to the content of the reading.

One takeaway from these perspectives is the role of explicitness in teaching with writing. In all cases, faculty in our study were easily able to articulate the ways writing worked in their classes, the importance they saw for disciplinary writing, and the challenges and triumphs they faced repeatedly in their work with students. Their range of confidence with these practices varied to some degree, but clear articulation of the intersection of the key factors that contribute to meaningful writing was consistent. This explicitness was noted by several of our undergraduate researchers as they reflected on their faculty interviews:

- Professor G__ is one of the only professors who goes into detail about what constitutes a strong thesis, and most students are surprised and challenged.

- What seemed most important during this interview was his outlook on what made the projects he assigns in his class most meaningful. He believes that what is most important is allowing the student to write what they want to write with few restrictions. I also found the setup of his class to be really important with what makes his assignments meaningful. His syllabus is very clear and direct so as he himself said, "If you want an A you will get one."

Of course, it does occur to us that the act of *asking* about these issues in our survey and interviews offers occasions for faculty to reflect on their practices, an occasion unfortunately rare in the teaching-research-and-service lives of university faculty.

It is also clear to us that these practices create opportunities for student agency, for engagement with others and with course material, and for learning for transfer. As we have pointed out previously, not all these outcomes happen simultaneously or in equal measure; the meaningful writing project is instead a learning space in which faculty and student intentions meet.

We also must note that we cannot offer a script or prescription for making an assignment meaningful to students. We have identified the key elements students and instructors described in our research, but the social and rhetorical practices assignments represent resist codified "rules"; student-teacher interaction is a social practice that, like all social practices, is subject to the many factors that govern human interactions. We can shed light on possibilities here and continue to work toward the meaningful writing project as a meeting place of faculty and student intention, hopes, and aspirations. In our final chapter, we offer some concluding thoughts on engaging in that work.

6
SOME CONCLUSIONS

In the preceding chapters, we describe the components necessary to foster meaningful writing experiences for students. While what we found is not complicated, neither is it a matter of solving a simple equation or providing a recipe. Meaningful writing happens for a reason, with intentions toward learning coming from both student and faculty, and is built on a platform that offers opportunities to amplify agency, engagement, and learning for transfer. To make writing agentive, relevant, and consequential, projects can be designed to cultivate personal connection, relations to future selves, and the disposition for lifelong learning. At the end of this chapter, we offer specific ideas for how this can happen, but first we offer some reflections on what we did and what we found.

Considering all of the data, all of the analysis, and all of the discussions we have had with each other and with groups of faculty and students across the country over the past four years, we think what we offer here is a good-news story: students are writing across their undergraduate years, in their majors, in general education courses, and outside class. When asked, they can tell us about a meaningful writing experience (only 4 percent of students who took the survey reported *none*). It could be that asking our question offered a (rare) reflective opportunity, one that allowed students to perhaps for the first time articulate what they did know they knew about their own learning and becoming. In other words, taking part in our study gave students an opportunity to make meaning, just as we saw their meaningful writing projects do.

Our findings also affirm those who teach with writing in disciplines beyond writing studies and even in contexts without formal writing requirements, given the varied disciplinary locations (STEM, humanities, social sciences) of students in our study. We have seen through students' perspectives that meaningful writing happens

- in large classes,
- in small classes,
- in capstones,

DOI: 10.7330/9781607325802.c006

- in electives,
- in required classes,
- in general education classes,
- in humanities classes,
- in social science classes,
- in STEM classes,
- in laboratories,
- in independent studies,
- with other students/in group projects,
- with faculty at all ranks, full- and part-time
- with friends and family,
- without teachers,
- without grades/despite few incentives,
- without classrooms,
- through reflection,
- through deliberate planning.

We were impressed but not surprised that there is so much writing going on across disciplines through assignments informed by disciplinary practices and discourses but made accessible to students, at just the right time and place in their education. This is not magic, however. There seems to be a set of basic components set up in such a way (and there is no one way) as to invite students to be active participants in constructing a writing experience that involves more than just writing. It is tempting to connect the dots between faculty intentions and student experience and credit the assignment. However, as we unpacked the meanings from the data, it became important to break linear thinking—that good old school-based directionality of instructor gives assignments/students do them. The complexities of epistemologies and pedagogies are mostly hidden from us as researchers and from the instructors themselves. We reminded ourselves often to keep the focus on the students, whether in the research itself, the analysis of our data, or in what we chose to write about in this book.

We also started with students because we wanted students' voices and experiences to tell us what meaningful writing means. It was no surprise, then, when agency, engagement, and transfer emerged from the coding process because many of us are thinking about how to support agency, engagement, and transfer if we are working at the intersection of learning and teaching. But our work with our data pushed the familiar notions of agency (individual), engagement (self-directed), and transfer (transactional) into a more "expansive" frame (Engle et al. 2012):

agency now included both the personal and social; we saw engagement occurring with self, others, and things; and we flipped the prevailing talk from teaching for transfer to learning for transfer.

Research on teaching is filled with calls to listen to students' lived experiences, and while our students' responses were all delivered retrospectively, they can inform our practices today. Alison Cook-Sather (2009) calls for more of us to work toward "gaining access to those perspectives":

> Treating students as legitimate informants on their learning experiences gives us access to what ethnographers call "meaning perspectives"—the perspectives from which students make meaning and thus influence any meaning made regardless of what works, what does not work, and what could work in their learning. Gaining access to those perspectives can help teachers make what they teach more accessible to students and make sure that what they teach is relevant. (239)

Though we do see some inclusion of student voices in research by composition and rhetoric scholars, it still remains that few studies across all disciplines "place student experience at the center of attention" (Cook-Sather 2009, 237), and thus few place students' experiences of writing at the center. Including students' perspectives aligns with constructivist ideas that students can and do make meaning for themselves. Our questions asked them to make meaning through stories or narratives, which aid in "understanding the past events of one's life and for forming future actions . . . meaning is found in the words themselves" (Polkinghorne 1988, 35).

We were also constantly reminded throughout our research that calls for learner-centered approaches to education—as opposed to teacher-centered—are not new. Over twenty years ago, Barr and Tagg (1995) claimed that higher education was experiencing a "paradigm shift" in the recognition that the goal was "to produce learning" rather than "provide instruction" (13). This focus on learning is elusive, however. As we point out in chapter 4, in trying to shift emphasis from teaching for transfer to learning for transfer, our institutions and often our writing programs are structured to favor curricular solutions, which are often driven by good intentions but also by assumptions about students that position them as passive recipients, not agentive actors able to determine their educational futures. We sincerely hope this book contributes to the shift to a learning paradigm; students can tell us a great deal about our efforts if we take the time to listen.

Some may ask, so what if a student says something is meaningful? What about the quality of the product? The writing ability? Well, we

don't privilege product—we are more interested in the student's con-
struction of meaning, for themselves. With few exceptions, faculty in
our study also did not privilege the text-based product over the whole
experience, which may have included field work, primary research, new
genres, personally significant prompts, and so forth. But it is not just
that faculty can (and maybe should) set assignment parameters that
require students to work in these ways—asking students explicitly to tap
into personal connection or find relevance. What seems key to us is that
faculty can also set assignment parameters with enough student choice
and enough encouragement of student agency that students may *choose*
to take up the invitation, and, if allowed and further encouraged, will
bring the power of personal connection, future relevance, and deep
immersion to what they're thinking, writing, and researching. But students must feel invited and encouraged. Constructing assignments that
elicit more meaningful results will require some intentionality, and,
likely, a closer look at what our assignments might actually be doing, a
closer look at the boundaries.

We also don't believe the meaningful writing project rests on one factor. What we can say is that the kinds of assignments or opportunities
offered seem to recognize writing as a social act, meaning that although
completed individually, the student is able to operate in a socially influenced environment much larger than the assignment but prompted
by the "assignment." That environment is framed expansively (Engle
et al. 2012), optimizing all the points of connection between student
and opportunity to write. Intentions and motivations cohere around
the meaningful writing project itself; it is not the student alone or the
assignment alone—meaning does not reside in one or the other. It is
found in the location of opportunities. And our study's interactions with
faculty confirm Beyer, Taylor, and Gillmore's (2013) finding that "professors who were passionate about their subject areas and who demonstrated that they cared about students' learning" were the most important factors in student learning (345). Such findings echo the 2014
Gallup-Purdue Index Report in that participants were twice as likely to
be engaged in their work postgraduation if they had "at least one professor . . . who made [them] excited about learning" ("Great Jobs, Great
Lives: The 2014 Gallup-Purdue Index Report" 2014, 10) during their
time as undergraduates. What would it look like if we shared our passion
for the subject more explicitly, viewing our teaching and writing assignments as connections to content? And what if we consistently viewed our
writing assignments as building potential connections to one another
and the world?

Even when a student's meaningful writing project was high stakes and clearly meant to be academic writing in what we might commonly think of in its most restrictive forms, is it possible that its comparative meaningfulness is due to a less "regulatory" assignment design, one that does not "restrict access" to the discourses students might choose (Lillis 2002)? Lillis (2002) notes the ongoing "tensions between individual desire and institutional regulation of meaning making" (161); perhaps we view that tension as a space that offers opportunities to reconcile what students want, want to do, and want to write about with faculty intentions to support both student development and assessment. But to turn the tension to a space that offers opportunities requires attention to and fostering of all we've described here via student experiences.

An important body of literature argues we should be paying attention not just to reading and writing in school as we know it but to the multiple literacies in students' lives. Scholars invested in this work across a number of contexts and from a number of different perspectives (e.g., Banks 2010; Guerra 2015; Kells 2007; Kirkland 2013; Leki 2007; Lunsford 2008; Palmeri 2012; Roozen 2010, 2012; Ruecker 2015; Shipka 2013, to name only a few) rightfully remind us that our sense in higher education of what counts as literate activity is so narrow that we miss much, perhaps most, of what makes composing in our students' literacy lives (in all our lives) so rich, so full, and so meaningful. The findings from research on student literacy practices in the case study below resonate with our findings as well:

> Laura talked about the literacy practices that revealed a high degree of personal ownership and commitment. She indicated that she had in different ways "made her own" even the literacy practices related to college coursework. But, more importantly, the literacy practices she deemed important seemed intimately connected to *both* who she said she was—a band member and a music student—and what she wanted to become—a songwriter/musician. Current contexts and imagined futures were both important to what she practiced and what she valued. (Ivanic et al. 2009, 171)

What would we need to pay attention to, or do, to make certain the writing students do for our classes is meaningful within school and in conjunction with all the other literacies of their lives?

We also need to note the rich data we collected in the course of this research that we have not presented, including many students' meaningful writing projects themselves and many faculty members' assignment prompts for those projects. These documents are fascinating and bewildering, offering a range of texts that belies tidy categorizing. And the texts themselves seen in isolation do not tell us nearly as much as student and faculty descriptions of why these projects were meaningful or produced meaningful writing. While direct measures of student performance are commonly seen as the ideal form of assessing student achievement in writing, our study reinforced for us how any text contains multiple stories of intent and execution and how effective assessment must take into account the multiplicity of those stories.

As we conclude, what can we offer those of you reading the book? Perhaps it is helpful to engage in some "not" talk (Nowacek 2011). The Meaningful Writing Project is not about the assignments themselves (Melzer 2014), not about the writing skills, which we did not evaluate, and not about curriculum. What the Meaningful Writing Project is about, foremost, is how much more students can gain when we frame the writing activities we want them to do as expansively inviting. We (faculty, tutors, and mentors) have likely been underestimating our potential influence on student agency, engagement, and learning for transfer; you may assign that same project every semester, but to the student it is a one-time experience, and it could, with your intentionality built in, become their most meaningful writing project.

At times during the analysis process, we believed that the findings would be wrapped up in a metaphor that would help us see and describe the meaning of meaningful writing and how it comes to be. We were playing with ideas of openings and passageways or meeting spaces and mixtures (often with the same ingredients in different measure). Is the meaningful writing project a place, an invitation, a conveyance, an affordance, a cocktail, a portal, or a sliding door? At more than one of our presentations, participants compared a meaningful writing experience to a single, great love. But we reject the idea that there can be—or should be—only one meaningful writing project in a lifetime. We can't resist trying on a couple of our attempts just to show you what these metaphors are trying to say:

> *Maybe it is the difference between handing students a full bucket and handing students a bucket with a strong handle on it and encouraging them to fill it with whatever they choose to add . . . that affordance brings the student much more autonomy, support, confidence and choice of resources . . .*
>
> *We have lots of examples of faculty who offered an invitation . . . set the table . . . try to imagine you have set the table, but some might come in, sit down, and open their own lunchbox and use their own utensils . . .*

These suggest we began to view the project itself as an *opportunity*, its meaningfulness resulting from a connection between faculty and student aims, a connection which can more easily take place within an expansive learning framework (Engle et al. 2012). But we have struggled to see this expansive framing idea as metaphorical, as it seems much more real and substantial to us; we finally realized we had permission give up the search for the perfect metaphor; as King Beach (1999) figured out long before us in his research on transfer, it is better to "discard [using a] metaphor for what it is we are trying to understand and support" (30).

Our analysis does leave us with some ways to conceptualize what we can all do to make writing meaningful for undergraduate writers. If you teach, tutor, or mentor in any setting and in any discipline or profession, and you have the sense that students find the writing you ask them to do meaningful, we hope we have given you some explicit lenses and language for understanding and explaining what it is in your teaching that might provide opportunities for students to experience meaningful writing projects. In an attempt to be more specific, we also offer the following suggestions:

Ask your students reflective questions about what is meaningful in the writing they're doing for your courses and why. We will admit that as we have worked on this study, each of us has thought more deeply about these questions in our own teaching—and asked our students these questions more explicitly—than we think we ever have before. The results have been affirming, and at times, when we learned why our framing of writing in our pedagogy was working differently than we had understood or better than we had realized, baffling. But each of us has grown as a teacher because of living with our own "Why meaningful?" questions.

Look closely for the places where aspects of a writing assignment can be made more expansive, more inviting, more past connected and more future oriented in ways driven by students' goals and interests. Many of us in higher education strive to get to know our students and their experiences, interests, and goals in the course of a semester, believing that with that knowledge we may be able to more successfully mentor and advise our students' learning. But what runs through the majority of students' responses explaining why their writing projects were their most meaningful is a sense that something about a course and its content, a faculty member, or an opportunity to write allowed them to make agentive choices and connections for themselves. Most often this work was also supported, mentored, appreciated, and admired, usually by an instructor but sometimes by an additional literacy sponsor (Brandt 1998). When this happened, writing projects were no longer simply the textual transactions or writing whose primary purpose was to inform the instructor about what the student learned, the kind of writing tasks that made up 66 percent of what Melzer (2014) found in his study of writing assignments across the curriculum. We can't help but contrast what Melzer concludes about these writing tasks—"Most of the assignments with an informative purpose give students an extremely limited view of academic discourse, instead asking them to simply display the 'right' answer or the 'correct' definition to the instructor through a recall of facts" (22)—with the rich experiences students in our study reported.

Consider the meanings students can make and take with them beyond satisfying you through completing an assignment. Sometimes we are so worried about students fulfilling goals we want and need them to fulfill, and so focused on helping them meet those goals, we can forget our assignments echo beyond what we could have imagined or planned. This may be one of our more difficult conclusions because we can't promise any instructor will learn about the many meanings students carry away from writing projects. Some may have to be discovered by students retrospectively or invoked when needed in future moments of learning or writing. Others may be too private to share with an instructor. But we cannot stop thinking about students who described how writing about course content shed light on personal issues, or how exposure to new writing processes changed their relationship to writing, or how finding agency as a researcher and writer led them to commit to doing various kinds of good in their communities. What we know from this study is that writing projects are a space in which faculty can tell students they care that this kind of meaning making could happen, and when they do, students hear them and try to imagine what it could mean for them individually.

Think about the relationship between all of the very good, well-established writing-across-the-curriculum and writing-in-the-disciplines processes and practices we know and how these intersect with the ideas we have offered here. At one point in our analysis, we pulled out all the faculty survey responses about how writing works in their teaching we had identified as descriptions of teaching "practices." We saw a dizzying array of familiar practices named, from peer review to conferencing with students, to encouraging drafts and providing feedback, to various forms of revision and editing strategies and various informal writing exercises. If 24 percent of student-survey responses reflected writing *process* and *writing to learn* as a meaningful element, we think those responses signal a widespread adoption of what many consider best practices in the teaching of writing across the disciplines. And, as we describe in chapter 3, seniors' meaningful writing project experiences included more attention to writing processes and assignment expectations than did the experiences of their 2012 NSSE peers from across the United States. But what the meaningful writing project has taught us as faculty who support other faculty teaching with writing is that by framing the opportunities for writing in their classes expansively, faculty can maximize the effects of the writing-across-the-curriculum and writing-in-the-disciplines strategies already so well documented and reinforced in Anderson et al.'s (2015) study of the National Survey of Student Engagement writing-question results, as we describe in chapter 3. If it seems as if we are being too vague here, go back to any or all of the case studies in chapters 2, 3 and 4 of this book, and/or to the stories from student and faculty perspectives in chapter 5, and we believe what we are saying will be obvious: students didn't find their projects meaningful only because they worked through drafts, for example, and were able to hone their arguments. They found them meaningful because their faculty supported them as they developed the arguments they wanted to make, imagined where they might want to take those arguments in the future, and encouraged their positions and their goals. We heard students recount their lengthy and somewhat excruciating experiences with editing as their answer to "Why meaningful," but they also described the care they felt their professor took to help them craft what they wanted to say as they wanted to say it. Others invoked peer review or peer workshops that were as awkward as we know they can be, but students were left valuing faculty who created and nurtured a space for varied perspectives of authorship in discussion, content learning, and writing. Seniors were able to say retrospectively that in informal writing they found connection to new content learning they had not expected, which led them to resee their past experience and reimagine their personal and professional futures. We know as faculty it is difficult to envision this result during the semester when we have no immediate evidence it is happening, but we strongly encourage you to assign and support students' writing because students told us they could feel when their mentors' pedagogy grew from a philosophy of connecting processes and practices to student learning.

Recognize the moments in writing center sessions and writing conferences with students when questions can move students to make connections with current and future selves. All three of us—and many others—have written about the ways in which writing centers can become regulatory, just another space in which students are encouraged to work to meet the dominant expectations of higher education (e.g., Boquet 1999; Geller et al. 2007; Grimm 1999; Lerner 2007; Lillis 2002; Melzer 2014). The Meaningful Writing Project has reminded us, so we hope it reminds those who educate tutors and writing center consultants, of the different types of questions students can be asked when they are sitting with content tutors in learning centers and writing consultants in writing centers. Rather than, Do you think this is meeting your professor's assignment?, the question could be, What is your professor hoping you will learn and do in this assignment, and what are you hoping to learn and do? Rather than saying to a student who is not connecting with a prompt, "Well, let's see what we can do to get it done," a tutor might say, "Have you ever thought about this before? Can you imagine any time you'll think about this again? How might something from your own experience help you complete this assignment?"

The writing center consultants who worked on this project as undergraduate researchers were very experienced, yet even they were surprised to hear from the students they interviewed when and how those students came to find meaning in projects. Sharing an excerpt of this book alongside our student-interview protocol with writing center and learning center tutors might prompt your tutor cohort to come up with their own strategies for applying the principles of the Meaningful Writing Project when tutoring their peers.

Even after completing our four-year investigation, there are some questions we have yet to answer: What factors account for some students realizing meaningful goals through their writing projects while others do not/cannot? How does race, gender, class, ability, and other factors intersect with students' experiences of meaningful writing? Would even more varied educational contexts affect responses to our "Why meaningful?" question? Our participants were all graduating from four-year institutions (although some cited meaningful writing projects written at other schools before transferring into one of our institutions). What would students say about their most meaningful writing project in two-year community college settings or in military academies or culinary institutes? How would high-school students describe their most meaningful writing experiences? We invite readers to take up these questions, whether using our survey or your own version, and contribute to an ongoing discussion of how, why, when, and where students find meaning in their writing.

In the end, we're left thinking about a central message of this research—meaningful writing projects are powerful because of the opportunities they offer. We close with a few more students describing why their projects were meaningful; we think you will see here exemplars both profound and mundane, but we hope their words act as a reminder that the scope of what we heard from students was exciting and affirming. Learning, teaching, and writing can become simultaneously more connected to our goals as educators and more connected to students' goals as learners if we value where students might choose to take their writing and why they might make those choices—allowing them the agency to make those choices and encouraging them to take hold of who they have been, who they are, and who they want to be in their futures.

> I was able to retell a meaningful holiday experience from my childhood while practicing both my Spanish and my writing skills in general.

> First of all, this paper was to be on a topic of my choosing, and I created this one, which makes it more personal and exciting from the start. But also, I believe that, much like in the era of the Depression, we are at a crossroads that requires a fundamental shift in how we think about national success. Subjective indicators are being adapted for Western use all the time, and the UN just endorsed the movement away from GDP alone in favor of a more comprehensive and subjective measurement of capability and prosperity. So, this topic is immediately relevant both to me and to the Western world.

> It initially seemed to be a daunting task. The amount of research I did was more than for any other assignment I've ever done. Thinking critically about such a broad real world problem, and trying to formulate my own solution was an invaluable experience. Having such a broad concept to study seemed impossible at first, but actually was a good thing because it forced me to consider so many different theorists and ideas as I formulated my own thoughts on the question.

> This project is meaningful to me because it gave me insight into who I am as a person and why I am the way I am. As a college student, you seldom get time to stop and think about where you have been, where you are, or where you are going. This assignment gave me the opportunity to do so.

APPENDIX A
Student Survey

St. John's University
Northeastern University
The University of Oklahoma

SENIORS REFLECT ON THEIR MEANINGFUL WRITING EXPERIENCES: A CROSS-INSTITUTIONAL STUDY

I'm a student at _____ . (REQUIRED)

St. John's University
Northeastern University
The University of Oklahoma

REQUEST TO PARTICIPATE IN RESEARCH

Consent Form For St. John's University

I would like to invite you to participate in a web-based online survey. The survey is part of a research study whose purpose is to gain an understanding of the elements that college students believe make writing tasks meaningful. In addition to St. John's University students at Northeastern University in Massachusetts and at the University of Oklahoma are also being asked about their meaningful writing experiences. This survey should take about 20 minutes to complete.

I am asking you to participate in this study because you are scheduled to graduate St. John's University in 2012. You must be at least 18 years old to take this survey.

The decision to participate in this research project is voluntary. You do not have to participate and you can refuse to answer any question. Even if you begin the web-based online survey, you can stop at any time.

There are no foreseeable risks or discomforts to you for taking part in this study.

DOI: 10.7330/9781607325802.c007

There are no direct benefits to you from participating in this study. However, your responses will give you an opportunity to reflect on your undergraduate education and the role of writing in that experience. Your responses will also potentially help improve the teaching of writing at St. John's and beyond.

All survey participants will be enrolled in a lottery to win $50 meal credit applied to your StormCard. Four $50 meal credits will be awarded.

Your part in this study is anonymous to the researcher(s). However, because of the nature of web based surveys, it is possible that respondents could be identified by the IP address or other electronic record associated with the response. Neither the researcher nor anyone involved with this survey will be capturing those data. Any reports or publications based on this research will use only group data and will not identify you or any individual as being affiliated with this project.

If you have any questions about this study, please feel free to contact Dr. Anne Ellen Geller at gellera@stjohns.edu, the Principal Investigator.

If you have any questions regarding your rights as a research participant, please contact the St. John's University Institutional Review Board (IRB), Newman Hall, Room 108, Queens Campus, 718-990-1440. You may call anonymously if you wish.

Please print out a copy of this consent form for your records.

Thank you for your time.

Dr. Anne Ellen Geller Department
of English St. John's University

I have read and understood the information above and am granting my informed consent for my participation in this research. (REQUIRED)

Yes, I agree   No, I decline

Consent Form for Northeastern University

I would like to invite you to participate in a web-based online survey. The survey is part of a research study whose purpose is to gain an understanding of the elements that college students believe make writing tasks meaningful. In addition to Northeastern, students at St. John's University in New York and at the University of Oklahoma are also being asked about their meaningful writing experiences. This survey should take about 20 minutes to complete.

I am asking you to participate in this study because you are in your final semester before graduation at Northeastern. You must be at least 18 years old to take this survey.

The decision to participate in this research project is voluntary. You do not have to participate and you can refuse to answer any question. Even if you begin the web-based online survey, you can stop at any time.

There are no foreseeable risks or discomforts to you for taking part in this study.

There are no direct benefits to you from participating in this study. However, your responses will give you an opportunity to reflect on your undergraduate education and the role of writing in that experience. Your responses will also potentially help improve the teaching of writing at Northeastern and beyond.

All survey participants will be enrolled in a lottery to win a $50 Amazon gift card. Four total gift cards will be awarded.

Your part in this study is anonymous to the researcher(s). However, because of the nature of web based surveys, it is possible that respondents could be identified by the IP address or other electronic record associated with the response. Neither the researcher nor anyone involved with this survey will be capturing those data. Any reports or publications based on this research will use only group data and will not identify you or any individual as being affiliated with this project.

If you have any questions regarding electronic privacy, please feel free to contact Mark Nardone, IT Security Analyst via phone at 617-373-7901, or via email at privacy@neu.edu.

If you have any questions about this study, please feel free to contact Neal Lerner at n.lerner@neu.edu, the Principal Investigator.

If you have any questions regarding your rights as a research participant, please contact Nan C. Regina, Director, Human Subject Research Protection, 960 Renaissance Park, Northeastern University, Boston, MA 02115. Tel: 617-373-7570, Email: irb@neu.edu. You may call anonymously if you wish.

Please print out a copy of this consent form for your records.

Thank you for your time.

> Dr. Neal Lerner Department of English
> Northeastern University

I have read and understood the information above and am granting my informed consent for my participation in this research. (**REQUIRED**)

Yes, I agree   No, I decline

Consent Form for The University of Oklahoma

I would like to invite you to participate in a web-based online survey. The survey is part of a research study whose purpose is to gain an understanding of the elements that college students believe make writing tasks meaningful. In addition to OU, students at St. John's University in New York and at the Northeastern University in Boston are also being asked about their meaningful writing experiences. This survey should take about 20 minutes to complete.

I am asking you to participate in this study because you are in your final semester before graduation at OU. You must be at least 18 years old to take this survey.

The decision to participate in this research project is voluntary. You do not have to participate and you can refuse to answer any question. Even if you begin the web-based online survey, you can stop and exit at any time.

There are no foreseeable risks or discomforts to you for taking part in this study.

There are no direct benefits to you from participating in this study. However, your responses will give you an opportunity to reflect on your undergraduate education and the role of writing in that experience. Your responses will also potentially help improve the teaching of writing at OU and beyond.

All survey participants will be enrolled in a drawing to win a $50 Amazon gift card. Four total gift cards will be awarded.

Your part in this study is anonymous to the researcher(s). However, because of the nature of web based surveys, it is possible that respondents could be identified by the IP address or other electronic record associated with the response. Neither the researcher nor anyone involved with this survey will be capturing those data. Any reports or publications based on this research will use only group data and will not identify you or any individual as being affiliated with this project.

If you have any questions regarding electronic privacy, please feel free to contact Mario Rosas: mrosas@ou.edu.

If you have any questions about this study, please feel free to contact Michele Eodice, the Principal Investigator: phone: (405) 325-2937 or via email: meodice@ou.edu.

If you have any questions regarding your rights as a research participant, please contact the Institutional Review Board by phone: (405) 325-8110 or via email: irb@ou.edu.

By clicking on the survey link below you are indicating that you consent to participate in this study. Please print out a copy of this consent form for your records.

Thank you for your time.

Michele Eodice
The University of Oklahoma

I have read and understood the information above and am granting my informed consent for my participation in this research. (REQUIRED)

Yes, I agree   No, I decline

ST. JOHN'S UNIVERSITY–COLLEGE/SCHOOL: (REQUIRED)
St. John's College of Liberal Arts and Sciences
The School of Education
The Peter J. Tobin College of Business
College of Pharmacy and Allied Health Professions
College of Professional Studies
Other

NORTHEASTERN UNIVERSITY–COLLEGE: (REQUIRED)
College of Arts, Media and Design
College of Business Administration
College of Computer and Information Science
College of Engineering
Bouvé College of Health Sciences
College of Professional Studies
College of Science
College of Social Sciences and Humanities
Other

THE UNIVERSITY OF OKLAHOMA–COLLEGE: (REQUIRED)
College of Allied Health
College of Architecture
College of Arts and Sciences
College of Atmospheric & Geographic Sciences
Michael F. Price College of Business
Mewbourne College of Earth and Energy
Jeannine Rainbolt College of Education
College of Engineering

Weitzenhoffer Family College of Fine Arts
Gaylord College of Journalism and Mass Communication
College of Liberal Studies
College of Nursing
College of Pharmacy
College of Public Health
Other

DEMOGRAPHIC INFORMATION
RACE/ETHNICITY:

American Indian/Alaskan Native
Asian
Black/African American
Hispanic
Native Hawaiian/Other Pacific Islander
White/Caucasian
Two or more races
Unknown
Other:

GENDER:

Male   Female

AGE:

18–21
22–25
26–29
30 and over

WHAT IS YOUR?

Major(s):
Minor(s):

OVERALL GPA:

MAJOR GPA:

LANGUAGE(S) IN WHICH YOU ARE
FLUENT (CHECK ALL THAT APPLY):

	Reading	*Writing*	*Speaking*
English			
Arabic			
Chinese			
French			
German			
Japanese			
Korean			
Portugese			
Russian			
Spanish			
Other			
If 'Other,' please specify.			

In this research, we are exploring the following questions:

1. What are the qualities of meaningful writing experiences as reported by university seniors at three different types of institutions?

2. What might seniors' perceptions of their meaningful/valuable writing experiences tell us about students' learning?

In this survey, we ask a combination of open-ended and scaled questions to explore a writing project you believe was "meaningful"—either a project that was a part of coursework or a project completed for purposes outside of class. A writing "project" could include many types of texts, whether completed by you alone or in collaboration with other students. A project could also include multi-media or visual "texts."

We will also ask you at the end of the survey if you are willing to be contacted for a follow-up one-to-one interview and focus group so that we might learn more about your experience.

We believe completing this survey will give you an opportunity to reflect on your undergraduate education and the role of writing in that experience. It will also potentially improve the teaching of writing and contribute to what is known about how students make meaning of their undergraduate experiences and their writing experiences.

1. Think of a writing project from your undergraduate career up to this point that was meaningful for you and answer the following questions:

1.1 Describe the writing project you found meaningful.

1.2 What made that project meaningful for you?

1.3 For the project you've described as meaningful, had you previously written anything similar?

    Yes   No

1.3a If YES, describe that previous writing project.

1.4 For the project you've described as meaningful, are there ways in which this writing project might contribute to the kinds of writing you hope to do in the future (for example, in your career or professional life)?

    Yes   No

1.4a If YES, please describe and be specific.

1.4b If NO, please describe and be specific.

2. Considering the writing project you identified as meaningful, check ANY of the following items that describe the process you used to write it:

> Brainstormed (listed ideas, mapped concepts, prepared an outline, etc.) to develop your ideas before you started drafting your writing project
> Talked with your instructor or a supervisor/mentor to develop your ideas before you started drafting your writing project
> Talked with a classmate, friend, or family member to develop your ideas before you started drafting your writing project
> Received feedback from your instructor or a supervisor/mentor about a draft before finalizing your writing project
> Received feedback from a classmate, friend, or family member about a draft before finalizing your writing project
> Visited an on-campus writing or tutoring center to get help with your writing project before finalizing it
> Used an online tutoring service to get help with your writing project before finalizing it
> Proofread your final draft for errors before finalizing it
> Had an opportunity to reflect on your writing process while developing or finalizing the writing project

3. For the writing project you've identified as meaningful, check ANY of the following items that describe the kind of writing you did:

> Narrate or describe one of your own experiences
> Summarize something you read, such as articles, books, or online publications

Analyze or evaluate something you read, researched, or observed

Describe your methods or findings related to data you collected in lab or field work, a survey project, etc.

Argue a position using evidence and reasoning

Explain in writing the meaning of numerical or statistical data

Write in the style and format of a specific field (engineering, history, psychology, etc.)

Include drawings, tables, photos, screen shots, or other visual content into your written assignment

Create the project with multimedia (web page, poster, slide presentation such as PowerPoint, etc.)

Include the project as part of a portfolio that collects written work you completed for a class

Include the project as part of a portfolio that collects written work from more than one class

Submit the project to a student or professional publication (magazine, journal, newspaper, collection of student work, etc.)

3.1   Feel free to add any additional comments that describe the kind of writing you did, including any information about your project that was not fully covered by these questions.

4.   For the writing project you have described as meaningful, did you work on it independently or with others (i.e., a collaboratively written or group project)?

Written independently

Written as part of a group project

5.   For the writing project you have chosen as meaningful, was it written as a course assignment or was it not connected to a course? (REQUIRED)

As a course assignment

Not connected to a course (e.g., for yourself, for a club, or during employment)

6.   If the writing project you identified as meaningful was completed as a part of coursework, name the course and the instructor:

6.1   Title of course:

6.2   Instructor:

6.3   Department offering course:

6.4   I took this class (semester):   Fall   Spring   Summer

6.5   I took this class (year):

2008   2009   2010   2011   2012

Other:

6.6 I was:

Freshman   Sophomore   Middler   Junior   Senior

7. For course for which you wrote this project, was that course (Check ALL that apply).

In your major
In the Core or General Education courses at your university
A required course
An elective

8. What was the course format?

Online
Hybrid/Blended
Campus classroom
Other:

9. If the writing project you identified as meaningful was completed as a part of coursework, check ANY of the following items that describe the role your instructor played:

Provided clear instructions describing what they wanted you to do
Explained in advance what they wanted you to learn
Explained in advance the criteria they would use to grade your writing project
Provided a sample of a completed project written by the instructor or a student
Asked you to do short pieces of writing that they did not grade
Asked you to give feedback to a classmate about a draft or outline the classmate had written
Asked you to write with classmates to complete a group project
Asked you to address a real or imagined audience such as your classmates, a politician, non-experts, etc.

9.1 Feel free to add any additional comments that describe the kind of writing you did, including any information about your project that was not fully covered by these questions.

As a follow up to this survey the research team for this project hopes to conduct brief (no more than ½ hour) interviews with those who have responded to this survey in order to learn more about the meaningful writing experience(s) described here. If you are willing to be contacted for an interview, please provide contact information where we might reach you. Your name and contact information will be reported to the research team separately from your survey response in order to protect your anonymity.

Would you like to be contacted for a brief follow-up interview? (RE-QUIRED)

Yes   No

How should we contact you?

Name:

By email:

By phone:

Thank you for participating in the survey.

If you are interested in participating for a drawing, please click on the link below to provide your e-mail address.

E-MAIL ADDRESS FOR DRAWING

Please allow 6–8 weeks for an e-mail address to be randomly selected, the participant will be contacted to provide additional information in order to receive the gift card.

Your e-mail address for the drawing will be sent to a database not associated with the survey, to maintain the anonymity of your responses.

Thank you for your time.

APPENDIX B
Student-Recruitment E-mail

Northeastern University, Department of English
Name of Investigator(s): Dr. Neal Lerner
Title of Project: Seniors Reflect on Their Meaningful Writing Experiences: A Cross-Institutional Study

E-MAIL TO RECRUIT STUDENT PARTICIPANTS

Hello! I would like to invite you to participate in a web-based online survey. I am asking you to participate in this study because you are in your final semester before graduation at Northeastern. All survey participants will be enrolled in a lottery to win a $50 Amazon gift card. Four total gift cards will be awarded.

The survey is part of a research study whose purpose is to gain an understanding of the elements that college students believe make writing tasks meaningful. In addition to Northeastern, seniors at St. John's University in New York and at the University of Oklahoma are also being asked about their meaningful writing experiences. This survey should take about 20 minutes to complete.

The decision to participate in this research project is voluntary. You do not have to participate and you can refuse to answer any question. Even if you begin the web-based online survey, you can stop at any time.

There are no foreseeable risks or discomforts to you for taking part in this study. There are also no direct benefits to you from participating in this study. However, your responses will give you an opportunity to reflect on your undergraduate education and the role of writing in that experience. Your responses will also potentially help improve the teaching of writing at Northeastern and beyond.

If you have any questions about this study, please feel free to contact Neal Lerner, the Principal Investigator, at n.lerner@neu.edu or 617–373.2451.

DOI: 10.7330/9781607325802.c008

APPENDIX C
Undergraduate and Graduate Research Assistants

Table C.1. University of Oklahoma

Undergraduate Researchers		Graduate Researchers
Natalie Dickson	Randall Proctor II	Evan Chambers
Janny Gandhi	Tyler Rhoades	Michael Rifenburg
Gerald Green	Sofia Rossainzz	Shannon Madden
Raven Hill	Teresa Sciortino	
Jyotsna Koduri	Danielle Wierenga	
Andy Phan	Warren Wright	
Mariana Piedra		

Table C.2. St. John's University

Undergraduate Researchers		Graduate Researchers
Julie Amadeo	Sami Korgan	Daniel Dissinger
Maria Angelidis	Brendan Latimer	Cristina Migliaccio
Kimberly Avalos	Cara Messina	Cara Messina
Raymond Blattner	Sandra Nelson	
Anthony Braxton	Angelo Poukamissas	
Mairead Carr	Joselin Rivera Rodriguez	
Catherine Hurley	Bailey Robertson	
Dylan Kitts	Jack Wells	

Table C.3. Northeastern University

Undergraduate Researchers		Graduate Researchers
Kathleen Collins	Abby Lance	Kyle Oddis
Sara Collins	Rowena Lindsay	Jessica Pauszek
Joy Davis	Efi Narliotis	
Marielle Evangelista Filler	Debora Pacella	
Minh Hoang	Peter Roby	
Abigail Kehoe	Kate Schnell	
Jessica Kelly	Ella Wang	
Christina Kompson		

DOI: 10.7330/9781607325802.c009

APPENDIX D
Student-Interview Questions

INTRODUCTORY REMARKS

Thanks for participating: I just want to remind you quickly about what this research is about [written on consent form] . . . then please sign the consent form and please say on the digital recording that you consent to being recorded. ("Is it okay if I digitally record?")

[Overview the four areas of the interview—even though these won't necessarily come in order.]

In this interview, I'm going to ask you about the writing project you've chosen as meaningful, the process of writing it, the context you wrote it in, and a bit about your writing as an undergraduate more generally.

Do you have any questions before we start?

Asking About the Meaningful Writing Project

1. What was the project you described as meaningful?

2. Why did you write that project?

3. When did you write this project (as a freshman, sophomore, etc.)? For what class [be sure to ask students full name of class]? (If not for class, then for what outside of class activity?) Was that class in your major? In general education? Required or elective?

4. In our survey we asked—For the project you've described as meaningful, had you previously written anything similar?—and 80% of students who responded said they had not previously written anything similar. Is this true for you? If yes, tell me about that. If not, what was the previous project?

[Is there anything else you want to say about any of this?]

Asking about the Processes of Writing the Project

5. Talk me through your process of writing this project. What do you remember about that process? What parts would you change if you had a chance to go back (if not already mentioned)? Please tell me about the most frustrating and satisfying aspects of the process of writing that project.

DOI: 10.7330/9781607325802.c010

6.   While you were working on this project did you talk with anyone about it? What have you talked about when you have mentioned it since you completed the project?

7.   What grade did you receive on that writing project?
[Do you have anything else you'd like to say about any of this?]

Asking about the Class/Instructional Context

8.   93% of the students who responded to our survey said the project they found meaningful was written in a course. Is that true for you? If it wasn't written in a course, can you tell me about the context?

[*If written for a course]

9.   How many students were in the class in which you wrote this project?

10. Can you tell me something about how that class was taught? (Did the professor lecture? Was it discussion, etc.?)

11. What role did the instructor play in making this project meaningful for you?

12. What did the work around the meaningful writing project look like in class (e.g., instructor discussing assignment, workshopping, peer review, group work)?

13. Was there other writing in the class besides this project? Was there any relationship between the other writing and this project?
[Do you have anything else you'd like to say about any of this?]

Asking About Writing More Generally

14. What has been the role of writing for you as an undergrad at [institution]?

15. How does this meaningful writing project compare to other writing you've done as an undergrad? Why is this one meaningful in comparison?

16. 69% of the students who responded to our survey said there were ways in which this writing project might contribute to the kinds of writing they hope to do in the future (e.g., in your career or professional life). Is this true for you? Why or why not?
[Do you have anything else you'd like to say about any of this?]
[Also, you can certainly prompt the student/writer to say anything about writing out of school too.]

If the Student Brings or Has the Project:

17. Is there anything you'd want to show me in this project and/or tell me about while we're looking at this project together?

[Get copy and/or get student to e-mail it!]

FINAL REFLECTION

Is there anything I haven't asked you about in this interview that you might want to tell me about?

APPENDIX E
List of Codes

affect (enjoyment, excitement, pleasant, pain, safe)

app+ (application/relevancy/future/pragmatic/authentic/
professionalization)

audience (awareness of rhetorical situation)

citation/documentation

collaboration

content learning

creative

deepen/fragmentary

engagement (of prof/of students)

failure/limitations

length

metacognition (thinking about writing process)

milestone/accomplishment/gaining confidence

new/new appreciation/new attitude

personal connection (incomes and prior knowledge)

process (describes writing or research process/sequence as meaningful)

resee with academic or analytical lens (from outside of school to in school)

reflection/recognition (of turning-point experience)

researching to learn (use of sources)

time/timing/timeliness

transfer (strategies, skills, knowledge transferred to meaningful writing
project)

writing to learn (knowledge, skills, and process)/writing to think

writing to realize (something about oneself)/identity

DOI: 10.7330/9781607325802.c011

APPENDIX F
Faculty-Interview Questions

Thanks for participating: I just want to remind you quickly about what this research is about [written on consent form] . . . then please *sign the consent* form and please say on the digital recording that you consent to being recorded. ("Is it okay if I digitally record this interview?")

[Overview of parts of the interview—even though these won't necessarily come in order.]

In this interview I'm going to ask you about the writing project a student has chosen as meaningful, the process and context of developing this writing assignment, your own meaningful writing experiences, and a bit about your views on teaching writing in your discipline more generally.

Do you have any questions before we start?

Asking About the Meaningful Writing Project Assignment and Class Context

1. How did it feel that a student cited your assignment as leading to a meaningful writing project? What did it make you think? Why?

2. [present the background information: one sheet per interview] It says here the student cited this project for this reason—here's what we have of how the student described it, but in your words could you tell us about this assignment? [If needed, prompt with particular semester and year that student cited.]

    [If the instructor brings the assignment sheet, make sure the instructor is referring to it as you talk.]

3. [asking more about the assignment] Tell us the origin story of this assignment. What made you design this assignment in this way? While developing this assignment, did you talk with anyone about it? What do you want students to learn from that assignment? Was there other writing in the class besides this project? Was there any relationship between the other writing and this project?

DOI: 10.7330/9781607325802.c012

4. [asking about the class] What can you tell us about this particular class as you taught it that semester that might have contributed to students finding the writing assignment meaningful? What are your learning goals for this class? What role does writing play? Tell us about the class: is it for majors, elective, required, general ed? When do students typically take it and who are they? How many students were in the class? Was it primarily lecture? Lab? Discussion based? Seminar?

5. We would like you to tell us about the processes you and students use as they're writing this assignment. For example, do you conference with students, expect drafts, use peer review or offer peer review workshops? Do you provide feedback to drafts and to the final product?

6. What kinds of grades do students typically get on this assignment? How do you grade/what does your process of grading look like?

7. What's frustrating and satisfying about working with this particular assignment or type of assignment with students?

    [Do you have anything else you'd like to say about any of this?]

Asking about Their Meaningful Writing Experience and Their Teaching of Writing

8. Can you describe your most meaningful writing project as an undergraduate? Why was that project meaningful?

Asking about Views on Teaching Writing and Being a Writer Yourself

9. Could you tell us the story of your use of writing in your teaching? Has it changed from when you started? What are your influences? Why do you do what you do?

10. What can you tell us about the writing you are currently doing? Who are you as a writer now?

    [Do you have anything else you'd like to say about any of this?]

11. We'll now share with you the reasons the student gave us for choosing this project as most meaningful as well as what the student might have said about doing this kind of writing in the future [share survey responses]. Does this make you think about anything we've already talked about or does it make you think of anything else you'd want to say?

FINAL REFLECTION

Is there anything I haven't asked you about in this interview that you might want to tell me about?

REFERENCES

Ambrose, Susan A., Michael W. Bridges, Michele DiPietro, Marsha C. Lovett, and Marie K. Norman. 2010. *How Learning Works: Seven Research-Based Principles for Smart Teaching.* Hoboken, NJ: John Wiley & Sons.

Anderson, Paul, Chris M. Anson, Robert M. Gonyea, and Charles Paine. 2015. "The Contributions of Writing to Learning and Development: Results from a Large-Scale Multi-Institutional Study." *Research in the Teaching of English* 50 (2): 199–235.

Arum, Richard, and Josipa Roksa. 2011. *Academically Adrift: Limited Learning on College Campuses.* Chicago, IL: University of Chicago Press.

Banks, Adam Joel. 2010. *Digital Griots: African American Rhetoric in a Multimedia Age.* Carbondale: Southern Illinois University Press.

Barber, James P., Patricia M. King, and Marcia B. Baxter Magolda. 2013. "Long Strides on the Journey toward Self-Authorship: Substantial Developmental Shifts in College Students' Meaning Making." *Journal of Higher Education* 84 (6): 866–96. http://dx.doi .org/10.1353/jhe.2013.0033.

Barr, Robert B., and John Tagg. 1995. "From Teaching to Learning—A New Paradigm for Undergraduate Education." *Change: The Magazine of Higher Learning* 27 (6): 12–26. http://dx.doi.org/10.1080/00091383.1995.10544672.

Baxter Magolda, Marcia B. 1999. *Creating Contexts for Learning and Self-Authorship: Constructive-Developmental Pedagogy.* Nashville, TN: Vanderbilt University Press.

Baxter Magolda, Marcia B., and Patricia M. King. 2004. *Learning Partnerships: Theory and Models of Practice to Educate for Self-Authorship.* Sterling, VA: Stylus Publishing.

Bazerman, Charles. 1994. "Systems of Genres and the Enactment of Social Intentions." *Genre and the New Rhetoric,* edited by Aviva Freedman and Peter Medway, 79–101. Abingdon, UK: Taylor and Francis.

Beach, King. 1999. "Consequential Transitions: A Sociocultural Expedition beyond Transfer in Education." *Review of Research in Education* 24 (January): 101–39.

Beaufort, Anne. 2007. *College Writing and Beyond: A New Framework for University Writing Instruction.* Logan: Utah State University Press.

Bennett, Jane. 2001. *The Enchantment of Modern Life: Attachments, Crossings, and Ethics.* Princeton, NJ: Princeton University Press.

Berlin, James A. 1987. *Rhetoric and Reality: Writing Instruction in American Colleges, 1900–1985.* Carbondale: Southern Illinois University Press.

Beyer, Catharine Hoffman, Edward Taylor, and Gerald M. Gillmore. 2013. *Inside the Undergraduate Teaching Experience: The University of Washington's Growth in Faculty Teaching Study.* Albany: SUNY Press.

Bishop, Wendy. 1992. "I-Witnessing in Composition: Turning Ethnographic Data into Narratives." *Rhetoric Review* 11 (1): 147–58. http://dx.doi.org/10.1080/07350199209388993.

Blum, Susan. 2009. *My Word: Plagiarism and College Culture.* Ithaca, NY: Cornell University Press.

Bogdan, Robert, and Sari Knopp Biklen. 2006. *Qualitative Research for Education. An Introduction to Theories and Methods.* 5th ed. New York: Pearson.

Boquet, Elizabeth H. 1999. "'Our Little Secret': A History of Writing Centers, Pre- to Post-Open Admissions." *College Composition and Communication* 50 (3): 463–82.

DOI: 10.7330/9781607325802.c013

Brandt, Deborah. 1998. "Sponsors of Literacy." *College Composition and Communication* 49 (2): 165–85. http://dx.doi.org/10.2307/358929.

Bratman, Michael E. 2000. "Reflection, Planning, and Temporally Extended Agency." *Philosophical Review* 109 (1): 35–61. http://dx.doi.org/10.1215/00318108-109-1-35.

Bundick, Matthew J., Russell J. Quaglia, Michael J. Corso, and Dawn E. Haywood. 2014. "Promoting Student Engagement in the Classroom." *Teachers College Record* 116 (4): 1–34.

Canagarajah, S. 2013. *Translingual Practice: Global Englishes and Cosmopolitan Relations.* New York: Routledge.

Carroll, Lee Ann. 2002. *Rehearsing New Roles: How College Students Develop as Writers.* Carbondale: Southern Illinois University Press.

Close, Esther Hess. 1936. "Meaningful Communication." *English Journal* 25 (4): 310–11. http://dx.doi.org/10.2307/805018.

Cook-Sather, Alison. 2009. *Learning from the Student's Perspective: A Sourcebook for Effective Teaching.* Boulder, CO: Paradigm.

Cooper, Marilyn M. 2011. "Rhetorical Agency as Emergent and Enacted." *College Composition and Communication* 62 (3): 420–49.

Crowley, Sharon. 1998. *Composition in the University: Historical and Polemical Essays.* Pittsburgh, PA: University of Pittsburgh Press.

CWPA, NCTE, and NWP. 2011. *Framework for Success in Postsecondary Writing.* Council of Writing Program Administrators, National Council of Teachers of English, and National Writing Project. January. http://wpacouncil.org/files/framework-for-success-postsecondary-writing.pdf.

Dirkx, John M. 1998. "Transformative Learning Theory in the Practice of Adult Education: An Overview." *PAACE Journal of Lifelong Learning* 7:1–14.

Driscoll, Dana Lynn, and Jennifer Wells. 2012. "Beyond Knowledge and Skills: Writing Transfer and the Role of Student Dispositions." *Composition Forum* 26 (Fall). http://compositionforum.com/issue/26/beyond-knowledge-skills.php.

Emirbayer, Mustafa, and Ann Mische. 1998. "What Is Agency?" *American Journal of Sociology* 103 (4): 962–1023. http://dx.doi.org/10.1086/231294.

Engle, Randi A., Diane P. Lam, Xenia S. Meyer, and Sarah E. Nix. 2012. "How Does Expansive Framing Promote Transfer? Several Proposed Explanations and a Research Agenda for Investigating Them." *Educational Psychologist* 47 (3): 215–31. http://dx.doi.org/10.1080/00461520.2012.695678.

Fried, Jane. 2016. *Of Education, Fishbowls, and Rabbit Holes: Rethinking Teaching and Liberal Education for an Interconnected World.* Sterling, VA: Stylus.

Gallagher, Chris W. 2002. *Radical Departures: Composition and Progressive Pedagogy.* Urbana, IL: NCTE.

Gee, James Paul. 2004. *Situated Language and Learning: A Critique of Traditional Schooling.* New York: Psychology Press.

Geller, Anne Ellen. 2005. "First Year Students' Perception of Writing." Unpublished study, Clark University, Worcester, MA.

Geller, Anne Ellen. 2013. "How to Enhance Meaning-Centered Writing and Reading." In *Meaning-Centered Education: International Perspectives and Explorations in Higher Education,* edited by Olga Kovbasyuk and Patrick Blessinger, 140–53. London: Routledge.

Geller, Anne Ellen, Michele Eodice, Frankie Condon, Meg Carroll, and Elizabeth Boquet. 2007. *The Everyday Writing Center: A Community of Practice.* Boulder: University Press of Colorado.

Glaser, Barney G., and Anselm L. Strauss. 1967. *The Discovery of Grounded Theory: Strategies for Qualitative Research.* Chicago, IL: Aldine.

Grafton, Anthony. 2011. "Our Universities: Why Are They Failing?" *New York Review of Books,* November 24. http://www.nybooks.com/articles/2011/11/24/our-universities-why-are-they-failing/

"Great Jobs, Great Lives: The 2014 Gallup-Purdue Index Report." 2014. Indianapolis, IN: Lumina Foundation. https://www.luminafoundation.org/files/resources/galluppur dueindex-report-2014.pdf.

Grimm, Nancy Maloney. 1999. *Good Intentions: Writing Center Work for Postmodern Times.* Portsmouth, NH: Boynton/Cook.

Guerra, Juan. 2008. "Cultivating Transcultural Citizenship: A Writing across Communities Model." *Language Arts* 85 (4): 296–304.

Guerra, Juan C. 2015. *Language, Culture, Identity and Citizenship in College Classrooms and Communities.* London: Routledge.

Hass, Michael, and Jan Osborn. 2007. "An Emic View of Student Writing and the Writing Process." *Across the Disciplines* 4 (August).

Haswell, Richard H. 1991. *Gaining Ground in College Writing: Tales of Development and Inter-pretation.* Dallas, TX: Southern Methodist University Press.

Haswell, Richard H. 2005. "NCTE/CCCC's Recent War on Scholarship." *Written Communication* 22 (2): 198–223. http://dx.doi.org/10.1177/0741088305275367.

Herrington, Anne, and Marcia Curtis. 2000. *Persons in Process: Four Stories of Writing and Personal Development in College.* Urbana, IL: NCTE.

Hilgers, Thomas L., Edna L. Hussey, and Monica Stitt-Bergh. 1999. "'As You're Writing, You Have These Epiphanies': What College Students Say about Writing and Learning in Their Majors." *Written Communication* 16 (3): 317–53. http://dx.doi.org/10.1177/0 741088399016003003.

Hull, Glynda A., and Mira-Lisa Katz. 2006. "Crafting an Agentive Self: Case Studies of Digital Storytelling." *Research in the Teaching of English* 41 (1): 43–81.

Inoue, Asao B. 2015. *Antiracist Writing Assessment Ecologies: Teaching and Assessing Writing for a Socially Just Future.* Perspectives on Writing. Fort Collins, CO: WAC Clearinghouse and Parlor. http://wac.colostate.edu/books/inoue/.

Ivanic, Roz, Richard Edwards, David Barton, Marilyn Martin-Jones, Zoe Fowler, Bud-dug Hughes, Greg Mannion, Kate Miller, Candice Satchwell, and June Smith. 2009. *Improving Learning in College: Rethinking Literacies across the Curriculum.* London: Routledge.

Jarratt, Susan C., Katherine Mack, Alexandra Sartor, and Shevaun E. Watson. 2009. "Peda-gogical Memory: Writing, Mapping, Translating." *WPA: Writing Program Administra-tion—Journal of the Council of Writing Program Administrators* 33 (1–2): 46–73.

Kegan, Robert. 2000. "What 'Form' Transforms? A Constructive-Developmental Approach to Transformative Learning." In *Learning as Transformation: Critical Perspectives on a Theory in Progress,* edited by Jack Mezirow and Associates, 3–34. The Jossey-Bass Higher and Adult Education Series. San Francisco: Jossey-Bass Publishers.

Kells, M. H. 2007. "Writing across Communities: Deliberation and the Discursive Possibili-ties of WAC." *Reflections: The SoL Journal* 17 (1): 87–108.

Kirkland, David E. 2013. *A Search Past Silence: The Literacy of Young Black Men.* New York: Teachers College Press.

Kuh, George D. 2003. "What We're Learning about Student Engagement from NSSE: Benchmarks for Effective Educational Practices." *Change: The Magazine of Higher Learning* 35 (2): 24–32. http://dx.doi.org/10.1080/00091380309604090.

Kuh, George D. 2008. *High-Impact Educational Practices: What They Are, Who Has Access to Them, and Why They Matter.* Washington, DC: Association of American Colleges and Universities.

Kuh, George D. 2009. "What Student Affairs Professionals Need to Know about Student Engagement." *Journal of College Student Development* 50 (6): 683–706. http://dx.doi.org /10.1353/csd.0.0099.

Lawson, Michael A., and Hal A. Lawson. 2013. "New Conceptual Frameworks for Student Engagement Research, Policy, and Practice." *Review of Educational Research* 83 (3): 432–79. http://dx.doi.org/10.3102/0034654313480891.

Leki, Ilona. 2007. *Undergraduates in a Second Language: Challenges and Complexities of Academic Literacy Development*. London: Routledge.

Lerner, Neal. 2007. "Rejecting the Remedial Brand: The Rise and Fall of the Dartmouth Writing Clinic." *College Composition and Communication* 59 (1): 13–35.

Lett, James. 1990. "Emics and Etics: Notes on the Epistemology of Anthropology." In *Emics and Etics: The Insider/Outsider Debate*, edited by Thomas N. Headland, Kenneth L. Pike, and Marvin Harris, 127–42. Thousand Oaks, CA: Sage.

Light, Richard J. 2004. *Making the Most of College: Students Speak Their Minds*. Boston, MA: Harvard University Press.

Lillis, Theresa M. 2002. *Student Writing: Access, Regulation, Desire*. New York: Routledge.

Lindenman, Jessica. 2015. "Inventing Metagenres: How Four College Seniors Connect Writing across Domains." *Composition Forum* 31 (Spring). http://compositionforum.com/issue/31/inventing-metagenres.php.

Lunsford, Andrea A. 2008. "The Stanford Study of Writing." Stanford, CA: Stanford University. http://ssw.stanford.edu/.

Maslow, Abraham. 1967. "Self-Actualizing and Beyond." In *Challenges of Humanistic Psychology*, edited by James F. T. Bugental, 118–32. New York: McGraw-Hill.

Melzer, Dan. 2014. *Assignments Across the Curriculum: A National Study of College Writing*. Logan: Utah State University Press.

Miller, Carolyn R. 1984. "Genre as Social Action." *Quarterly Journal of Speech* 70 (May): 151–67.

Moje, Elizabeth B., and Cynthia Lewis. 2007. "Examining Opportunities to Learn Literacy: The Role of Critical Sociocultural Literacy Research." In *Reframing Sociocultural Research on Literacy: Identity, Agency, and Power*, edited by Cynthia Lewis, Patricia E. Enciso, and Elizabeth Birr Moje, 15–48. New York: Routledge.

Moje, Elizabeth Birr, Katherine McIntosh Ciechanowski, Katherine Kramer, Lindsay Ellis, Rosario Carrillo, and Tehani Collazo. 2004. "Working Toward Third Space in Content Area Literacy: An Examination of Everyday Funds of Knowledge and Discourse." *Reading Research Quarterly* 39 (1): 38–70. http://dx.doi.org/10.1598/RRQ.39.1.4.

Moore, Jessie. 2012. "Mapping the Questions: The State of Writing-Related Transfer Research." *Composition Forum* 26 (Fall). http://compositionforum.com/issue/26/map-questions-transfer-research.php.

National Survey of Student Engagement (NSSE). 2008. "Promoting Engagement for All Students: The Imperative to Look Within: 2008 Results." http://nsse.indiana.edu/NSSE_2008_Results/docs/withhold/NSSE2008_Results.pdf.

National Survey of Student Engagement (NSSE). 2012. "Promoting Student Learning and Institutional Improvement: Lessons from NSSE at 13: Annual Results 2012." http://nsse.indiana.edu/NSSE_2012_Results/pdf/NSSE_2012_Annual_Results.pdf.

Nowacek, Rebecca. 2011. *Agents of Integration: Understanding Transfer as a Rhetorical Act*. Carbondale: Southern Illinois University Press.

Paine, Charles, Chris M. Anson, Robert M. Gonyea, and Paul Anderson. 2015. "Using National Survey of Student Engagement Data and Methods to Assess Teaching in First-Year Composition and Writing across the Curriculum." In *Assessing the Teaching of Writing: Twenty-First Century Trends and Technologies*, edited by Amy E. Dayton, 171–86. Logan: Utah State University Press. http://dx.doi.org/10.7330/9780874219661.c011.

Palmeri, Jason. 2012. *Remixing Composition: A History of Multimodal Writing Pedagogy*. Carbondale: Southern Illinois University Press.

Perkins, David N., and Gavriel Salomon. 1989. "Are Cognitive Skills Context-Bound?" *Educational Researcher* 18 (1): 16–25.

Perkins, David N., and Gavriel Salomon. 1992. "Transfer of Learning." *International Encyclopedia of Education* 2: 6452–57.

Perkins, David N., and Gavriel Salomon. 2012. "Knowledge to Go: A Motivational and Dispositional View of Transfer." *Educational Psychologist* 47 (3): 248–58. http://dx.doi.org/10.1080/00461520.2012.693354.

Poe, Mya. 2013. "Re-framing Race in Teaching Writing across the Curriculum." *Across the Disciplines* 10 (3). Accessed December 6, 2016. http://wac.colostate.edu/atd/race/poe.cfm.

Poe, Mya, Neal Lerner, and Jennifer Craig. 2010. *Learning to Communicate in Science and Engineering: Case Studies from MIT.* Boston: MIT Press.

Polkinghorne, Donald E. 1988. *Narrative Knowing and the Human Sciences.* Albany: SUNY Press.

Roozen, Kevin. 2012. "Comedy Stages, Poets Projects, Sports Columns, and *Kinesiology 341*: Illuminating the Importance of Basic Writers' Self-Sponsored Literacies." *Journal of Basic Writing* 31 (1): 99–132.

Roozen, Kevin. 2010. "Tracing Trajectories of Practice: Repurposing in One Student's Developing Disciplinary Writing Processes." *Written Communication* 27 (3): 318–54.

Roozen, Kevin. 2009. "'Fan Fic-ing' English Studies: A Case Study Exploring the Interplay of Vernacular Literacies and Disciplinary Engagement." *Research in the Teaching of English* 44 (2): 136–69.

Ruecker, Todd. 2015. *Transiciones.* Boulder: University Press of Colorado.

Saldaña, Johnny. 2015. *The Coding Manual for Qualitative Researchers.* Thousand Oaks, CA: SAGE.

Seidman, Irving. 1998. *Interviewing as Qualitative Research: A Guide for Researchers in Education and the Social Sciences.* New York: Teachers College Press.

Shipka, Jody. 2013. "Including, but Not Limited to, the Digital: Composing Multimodal Texts." In *Multimodal Literacies and Emerging Genres in Student Compositions*, edited by Tracey Bowen and Carl Whithaus, 73–89. Pittsburgh, PA: University of Pittsburgh Press.

Smagorinsky, Peter. 2008. "The Method Section as Conceptual Epicenter in Constructing Social Science Research Reports." *Written Communication* 25 (3): 389–411. http://dx.doi.org/10.1177/0741088308317815.

Smit, David W. 2004. *The End of Composition Studies.* Carbondale: Southern Illinois University Press.

Smitherman, Geneva, and Victor Villanueva. 2003. *Language Diversity in the Classroom: From Intention to Practice.* Carbondale: Southern Illinois University Press.

Sommers, Nancy, and Laura Saltz. 2004. "The Novice as Expert: Writing the Freshman Year." *College Composition and Communication* 56, 1 (September): 124–49.

Sternglass, Marilyn S. 1997. *Time to Know Them: A Longitudinal Study of Writing and Learning at the College Level.* Mahwah, NJ: Lawrence Erlbaum.

Strauss, Susan, and Xuehua Xiang. 2006. "The Writing Conference as a Locus of Emergent Agency." *Written Communication* 23 (4): 355–96. http://dx.doi.org/10.1177/0741088306292286.

Stenberg, Shari J. 2015. *Repurposing Composition: Feminist Interventions for a Neoliberal Age.* Boulder: University Press of Colorado.

Thaiss, Chris, and Terry Myers Zawacki. 2006. *Engaged Writers Dynamic Disciplines.* Portsmouth, NH: Boynton/Cook.

Wardle, Elizabeth. 2007. "Understanding 'Transfer' from FYC: Preliminary Results of a Longitudinal Study." *Writing Program Administration* 31 (2): 65–85.

Wardle, Elizabeth. 2012. "Creative Repurposing for Expansive Learning: Considering 'Problem-Exploring' and 'Answer-Getting' Dispositions in Individuals and Fields." *Composition Forum* 26 (1). http://compositionforum.com/issue/26/creative-repurposing.php.

Wenger, Etienne. 1999. "Communities of Practice: Learning as a Social System." *Systems Thinker* 9 (5): 2–3.

Yancey, Kathleen Blake. 1998. *Reflection in the Writing Classroom.* Logan: Utah State University Press.

Yancey, Kathleen Blake. 2011. "From the Editor: Writing Agency, Writing Practices, Writing Pasts and Futures." *College Composition and Communication* 62 (3): 416–19.

Yancey, Kathleen Blake, Liane Robertson, and Kara Taczak. 2014. *Writing across Contexts: Transfer, Composition, and Sites of Writing*. Logan: Utah State University Press.

Yin, Robert K. 2013. *Case Study Research: Design and Methods*. 5th ed. Thousand Oaks, CA: SAGE.

Zepke, Nick. 2014. "Student Engagement Research in Higher Education: Questioning an Academic Orthodoxy." *Teaching in Higher Education* 19 (6): 697–708. http://dx.doi.org/10.1080/13562517.2014.901956.

ABOUT THE AUTHORS

MICHELE EODICE is associate provost and director of the writing center at the University of Oklahoma. She is a coauthor of *Working with Faculty Writers*, *The Everyday Writing Center*, and *(First Person)²*.

ANNE ELLEN GELLER is associate professor of English and director of writing across the curriculum in the Institute for Writing Studies at St. John's University in Queens, New York. She is a coauthor of *Working with Faculty Writers* and *The Everyday Writing Center*.

NEAL LERNER is associate professor of English and writing program director at Northeastern University. He is the author of *The Idea of a Writing Laboratory*, winner of the 2011 NCTE David H. Russell Award for Distinguished Research in the Teaching of English, and a coauthor of *Learning to Communicate in Science and Engineering*, winner of the 2012 CCCC Advancement of Knowledge Award.

INDEX